Guide

H

CHES OF

BRITAIN

This book describes the wealth of history to be found in parish churches throughout Britain. The churches featured range from humble places of worship tucked away deep in the country to grand town-centre edifices, from ancient sites associated with early Christianity to extravagant buildings of the Victorian period. The story of each church is told in a fascinating way. The development of church architecture through the ages is fully described, and the book contains practical advice on what features to look for outside and within a church, and how to interpret what you see.

The book is divided into six geographic regions. Within each region, the places to visit are listed in alphabetical order.

About the author

Richard Foster is a writer and television producer specialising in architecture and art history. He studied first at Bath Academy of Art and later at the Royal College of Art. A major BBC film series *Discovering English Churches* was written and directed by the author. Recent work includes *The Secret Life of Paintings* for television, an examination of the hidden symbolic meaning of five late-medieval paintings written in collaboration with Pamela Tudor-Craig, and a book providing an in-depth study of the beautiful, but mysterious, 13th-century mosaic pavement before the high altar of Westminster Abbey.

ACKNOWLEDGEMENTS

The publishers gratefully acknowledge the following for the use of their photographs. Where more than one photograph appears on a page, credits are listed top and bottom. Many photographs were supplied by the Edwin Smith Photolibrary (designated ES in the credits), Janet and Colin Bord (JCB), the Royal Commission for Historic Monuments (RCHM) and Richard Foster (RF).

8. BBC Hulton Picture Library 18. RF (top left), JCB (top right) 19. RCHM 20, 21. Both JCB 22–4. All RF 25. AA Picture Library 26. A Besley 27. RF 28, 29. Both AA Picture Library 30. RF 31. RCHM 33, 34. Both ES 35. Both RCHM 36. Both JCB 37. RCHM 38. JCB (top left), ES (top right) 39. JCB 40. ES 41. RCHM 42. RF 43. ES 44. AA Picture Library 45. AF Kersting 46. RF, A Grierley 47, 48. Both RF 49–51. All ES 52. JCB 53. RCHM 54, 55. All RF 56. RCHM 57. JCB 58. AF Kersting 59. JCB 60, 61, 63, 64–7. All RF 68. RF, AA Picture Library 69. JCB 70. Both RF 71. ES 72. RCHM 73. RF 74. Both JCB 75. RCHM 76. ES 77. JCB 78–80. All RCHM 81. JCB 82. ES 83. JCB 84, 85. Both ES 86. RF 87, 88. Both AF Kersting 89. JCB 91. ES 92. JCB (top left), ES (top right) 93. Both JCB 94. AF Kersting 95. RCHM 96. EA Bowness 97. ES 98. RCHM 99. Kirkleatham Old Hall Museum 100, 101. All RCHM 102. ES 103. Richmond and Rigg 104, 105. Both ES 106. AA Picture Library 107. Both ES 108. St Giles's, Edinburgh (top left), ES (top right) 109. ES 110. AA Picture Library 111. ES 112. AA Picture Library 113. Scottish Development Department.

AA

Glovebox Guide

PARISH CHURCHES OF BRITAIN

Richard Foster

Produced by the Publishing Division
of The Automobile Association

F7567   Britain /

305310012466l8

OHIO CHRISTIAN UNIVERSITY

4

Editor: *Roger Thomas*
Art Editor: *Harry Williams FCSD*
Cover photograph: *Detail of window, Cartmel Priory,*
                      Rick Czaja, AA Photolibrary
Typesetting: *Afal, Cardiff*
Printing: *Purnell Book Production Ltd, a member of*
             the BPCC Group

The drawing on page 114 is based on an
illustration by Brian Delf in *Discovering English
Churches* by Richard Foster (BBC Books, 1981).

Produced by the Publishing Division of
The Automobile Association

Distributed in the United Kingdom by the
Publishing Division of The Automobile
Association, Fanum House, Basingstoke,
Hampshire RG21 2EA

The contents of this publication are believed
correct at the time of printing. Nevertheless, the
Publishers cannot accept responsibility for errors
or omissions, nor for changes to details given.

© The Automobile Association 1988, reprinted 1992

Cartography © The Automobile Association 1988

All rights reserved. No part of this publication
may be reproduced, stored in a retrieval system,
or transmitted in any form or by any means –
electronic, photocopying, recording, or
otherwise – unless the written permission of
the Publishers has been given beforehand.

ISBN 0 86145 682 3

Published by The Automobile Association

PARISH CHURCHES OF BRITAIN

Contents

It was a cold, east coast Easter when I first discovered that parish churches are more than picturesque back-drops for wedding photographs. Staying in the tiny village of Salthouse in Norfolk with the family of a fellow student, I was taken to see the church. The building was disproportionately large and grey, staring out blankly across an equally monochrome landscape towards the sea, the best part of a mile away. What need had such a small community ever had for a church of such size?

The clear glass windows, high and wide, suffused the interior with an even, bleaching light. My untutored eye searched in vain for some focus, some starting point. Then my friend's father, who happened to be a professor of recent archaeology, came to the rescue. He had disappeared on hands and knees behind the woodwork of the choir stalls. There, scratched in the ancient timbers, were graffiti of some three centuries ago — not just any graffiti, but a fleet of graceful sailing ships, cut perhaps by the idle hands of bored choirboys.

Here was the explanation for the church's disproportionate size: this village had once been a prosperous port with a navigable channel leading out to the trade routes with Europe. The ships were those that were then to be seen bobbing in the waters of the harbour. But over the centuries the sea receded, and the estuary silted up. The village declined and its church was left beached like a great grey whale.

This is one small example of what is writ large in British parish churches — if you know where to look, and how to read their language. For churches were not built in a day: they evolved over many generations, reflecting both the turning pages of national history and the particular lives of ordinary people. In the grandest of churches some gesture of spirited human individuality can usually be found within the standardised imagery and architecture associated with the medieval Church.

Walking into a church, our footsteps and our gaze tend automatically towards the altar. This is just the effect the church builders envisaged, of course. But in our hurry did we see the sundial scratched on the porch, the poor box inside the door, or the misericords in the chantry . . . ? The whats in the where? Ecclesiological terms can be obscure, and many a potential church-browser has been deterred by the language of the descriptive leaflets found in churches. So let's start again from the outside.

The first thing to look at is the churchyard. If it is circular, then the church is likely to be of very ancient foundation indeed, especially if it is set up on a mound like Edlesborough Church in Buckinghamshire. When the Christian missionaries came to Britain, they often built their churches on the sites of stone circles or man-made earthworks which were already considered holy ground by our pagan forbears. Rudston Church in Humberside still shares its churchyard with the country's tallest standing stone, a monolith almost 8m high. The gate into the churchyard may be covered with a roof, in which case it is called a lych gate, the name coming from the Old English word for a corpse, *lych*. Until modern times, only the wealthy could afford coffins: most people were buried in just a woollen or linen shroud. The lych gate is said to have sheltered the body from the elements until the priest arrived to lead the funeral procession.

The present church is seldom as old as its foundation: it is almost always either a partial or total rebuilding of an earlier church. But always make a thorough examination of the walls: they sometimes incorporate fragments of the original stonework, especially if it was attractively carved. Parts of a Saxon cross with a Celtic interlace pattern, for

example, or even a tomb slab, may be found in quite unexpected places. Doorways carved by Norman masons were particularly elaborate and were often retained even when the rest of the church was demolished. As you will have guessed by now, the question 'How old is this church?' is the easiest to ask, but usually ends up being the most complex to answer.

As you walk up to a church, its plan and general outline may give the first clue to its date — generally speaking, the simpler, the older. Before the Norman Conquest, a church was often divided into just two parts: the chancel at the east end which housed the altar and the priests, and the nave where the congregation stood.

This two-cell plan, as it is called, represents the fundamental division of the medieval church between the domains of the clergy and the laity. The chancel was separated from the nave by an arch, often rather narrow in Saxon churches. The archway was filled with a wooden screen called the chancel screen or the Rood screen since it usually supported a carving of Christ on the Cross which was known as the *Rood* in medieval times. The wall above the arch was often painted with a dramatic representation of the Last Judgement, called a Doom.

A porch was occasionally added around the south door, the normal entrance to the church, and possibly to the door on the north side too. After the Norman Conquest, the two-cell plan was

---

In describing church architecture, technical terms have been kept to an absolute minimum. If not explained in the text, they are listed in the glossary on pages 114—18 (see also the explanatory illustration of a complete church on page 114).

sometimes extended by inserting a third area between the chancel and nave to form a <u>three-cell plan</u>. The central section often supported an <u>axial tower</u>.

Detail from a medieval manuscript which shows stone masons at work

Important churches associated with monasteries were built with <u>aisles</u> on either side of the nave. They were separated from the central space by <u>arcades</u>, rows of <u>arches</u> supported on freestanding <u>piers</u>. As congregations grew after the Conquest, even ordinary parish churches needed extra space, so aisles were added by taking down the north and south nave walls. The north aisle is usually the older of the two for the practical reason that the south door was the main entrance to most churches and so it was less disruptive to build on the north side. Widening the church in this way made the centre of the nave darker. To increase the light, windows were pierced through the walls above the arcades to form a <u>clerestory</u>, literally a 'clear storey'.

For bigger churches, a <u>cruciform plan</u> became increasingly popular. The two arms to the north and south of this cross-shaped plan are called <u>transepts</u> and they might serve as chapels, sometimes for the exclusive use of a particular craft guild or noble family. A <u>central tower</u> was often built over the <u>crossing</u>, the meeting point of nave, transepts and chancel. In churches that were not built on a cruciform plan from the start, the tower was more commonly raised at the west end of the nave.

As both clergy and laity became more prosperous during the medieval period, south porches and transepts were added to many churches and the layout was further complicated by the building-on or fencing-off of <u>chantry chapels</u>. Chantries were endowed by rich patrons to provide themselves with a final resting place and to pay for a priest to say daily prayers for their souls. So the plan of a church as it stands today is often more the result of organic and sometimes haphazard evolution than the realisation of a master mason's blueprint. It is, therefore, usually wiser to date the parts of a church rather than its whole, and thereby gain an insight into its history. A 14th-century window inserted in a 12th-century wall and filled with 19th-century glass is not at all an unusual sight!

The architectural elements and fittings of a church — the shapes of windows, the forms of capitals, the carved decoration on doorways and arches, the design of screens and fonts — can usually be set in their architectural period by considering their style. Development in architectural styles reflected both innovation in tools and building techniques, and changes in aesthetic taste. Broadly speaking the pendulum of fashion in architecture has swung between two poles or opposing styles: <u>Classical</u> and <u>Gothic</u>.

The Classical style derived from the buildings of ancient Greece and Rome. Characterised by semicircular arches and round columns, this style spread across Europe in the footsteps of the Roman Empire and provided the model for early Christian buildings. After the fall of the Empire, local masons continued with Roman traditions but their work became infused with a more individual and flowing style, a distant echo of Rome revitalised with native Celtic and Viking influences. Churches of this style are called, appropriately, Romanesque. The Romanesque period was divided in two by the Norman Conquest, so the terms pre-Conquest Romanesque and Norman Romanesque are often used to distinguish between the Saxon and Norman types of building.

The second half of the 12th century brought a radical structural innovation which made possible an entirely new style of architecture: the style was Gothic, and the innovation the pointed arch. Because a pointed arch conducts the weight of the masonry it supports down to earth more efficiently than a semicircular one, it allowed walls and columns to be thinner. Churches were able to be built higher with taller and wider windows, which in turn brought the introduction of window tracery and stimulated the development of stained glass. At about the same time, the introduction of the chisel for stone carving, instead of the axe, meant that decoration could be finer and more deeply undercut. The massive character of Romanesque architecture with its vital but crude carving was replaced by a new lightness and delicacy.

Gothic architecture did not appear overnight of course: there were in fact several decades during which the old

and the new were used side by side, even in the same building. This period of change is marked by the Transitional style. But once the Gothic style had established itself, it was to reign supreme for more than three centuries.

When Gothic architecture was first seriously studied, in the 19th century, the architect and writer Thomas Rickman divided the period into three successive phases: Early English, Decorated and Perpendicular. These terms are still widely used today. Though descriptive, they may also be misleading: Early English was not exclusively English, for example, whereas Perpendicular was. In this book the more matter-of-fact terms Early Gothic, High Gothic and Late Gothic are preferred when describing the three phases of this glorious period in the history of church architecture.

The spirit of the Renaissance finally blew across the Channel during the 16th century, bringing with it many changes in aesthetic and intellectual attitudes. A renewed interest in the ancient worlds of Rome and Greece swung the pendulum of taste back to the Classical. In Britain, the Reformation provided an added impetus to turn away from what was now seen as the superstitious and ignorant Middle Ages, and to look towards the coming Age of Enlightenment. Unlike the Romanesque period, the Classical Revival produced architecture derived directly from classical models, its detail often copied accurately from Rome's actual ruins.

In church services the preaching of the sermon began to assume a greater importance than the Eucharist which was celebrated far less often than the medieval Mass. This shift in emphasis was reflected in the plan of new churches which were built on the auditory plan. The chancel shrank to insignificance and the nave became an open space dominated by the pulpit which was often raised up in three tiers. The congregation was seated in box pews arranged so that everyone in the church could clearly see and hear the all-important sermon.

Inevitably the pendulum swung back again, and the 19th century brought a renewed interest in medieval culture. At first it was merely a romantic interest in picturesque 'Gothik' ruins, but coupled with the High Church influence of the Tractarian Movement and the Cambridge Camden Society, it became a scholarly and emotional conviction that Gothic was the only truly Christian style of architecture, Classical being by definition irredeemably pagan. The architects of this Gothic Revival raised some of the best and the worst of our churches. Most were built in the growing manufacturing towns spawned by the Industrial Revolution. At worst, they were lifeless imitations of a bygone age. At best, the idealised Victorian view of medieval church builders found expression in wonderful purity of design realised with an extravagant confidence made possible by the country's industrial prosperity.

During the 20th century fewer parish churches have been built than in any other generation, with the possible exception of the years of the Civil War. In an age which makes little use of the Church, the struggle to maintain its existing buildings is a burden costly enough. Those new churches that have been built show the influence of the major movements in design, notably those associated with the Arts and Crafts Movement and Modernism.

So much for the sequence of church building styles. Now for some dates — and a warning. Masons did not wake up on the first day of 1300 to find a circular from their lodge informing them that Early Gothic was now out and High Gothic in. The division between one style and the next was not clear-cut, but blurred. Some masons were innovatory and led fashion, others lagged behind. Some patrons were rich and progressive, others poor and conservative. Not everything was made according to convention, of course, and the loveliest churches are often those where the mason has bent the rules or added his own spark of imagination. So bearing in mind that any division of medieval building into periods is an approximation, the architectural periods may be dated as follows:

Pre-Conquest Romanesque	600—1066
Norman Romanesque	1066—1160
Transitional	1160—1200
Early Gothic	1200—1300
High Gothic	1300—1350
Late Gothic	1350—1660
Classical Revival	1660—1830
Gothic Revival	1830—1900
Modern	1900—

PRE-CONQUEST ROMANESQUE (SAXON)

Most churches before the Conquest had rough rubble walls, thickly coated with a coarse plaster made of hair and straw mixed with sand and lime. Masonry of this period often reveals a distinctive herringbone pattern: the stones being laid diagonally in rows alternately sloping to the right and to the left, creating a zigzag effect. Extra strength was needed at the corners. Here, large vertical blocks were set alternately with flat horizontal slabs which penetrated

SAXON FEATURES

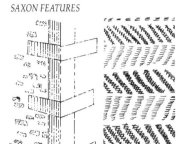

'Long and short' work   *Herringbone masonry*

and gripped the rubble walling. This technique is called 'long and short' work and, since it went out of fashion soon after the arrival of the Normans, is a fairly sure sign of pre-Conquest work.

The exterior of the walls was often decorated with thin, flat stone battens called pilaster strips or lesenes. They served no structural purpose. In some churches the pilaster strips simply divided the wall into bays, in others they were used to make a decorative geometric network which covered the whole surface.

Windows were usually small and set high up in the walls. Following the Roman fashion, many windows had semicircular arches at the top. But instead of being made up of separate wedge-shaped stones (voussoirs), they were often cut through one single large piece of stone. Windows are found in pairs, or occasionally in larger groups, with adjacent lights separated by a short shaft shaped like a wooden lathe-turned baluster. Triangular-headed windows are also found, formed by two stone slabs leaning together.

Doorways, too, were small and rather narrow in proportion to their height. Most had semicircular arches, sometimes with a concentric lesene over the top. Arcades were rare. Arches were invariably semicircular, and piers were short and squat, with primitive capitals and simple square bases, or none at all.

With a few notable exceptions, all pre-Conquest decoration was sparse. It was crudely chopped out with an axe and so had to be fairly simple in design and low in relief. Interlace patterns of Celtic tradition were carved by axe on crosses and shrines, but seem not to have been used in the fabric of buildings. Figure sculpture, especially the Rood group, was the main carved feature of the church interior.

NORMAN ROMANESQUE

The impression of mass and solidity that characterises churches built by the Norman conquerors is to some extent a sham: walls and piers that appear to be huge blocks of stone piled one upon the other are, in fact, built of rubble and faced with relatively thin squared slabs of stone called ashlar. When the patron could afford it, the masons preferred to use the Caen stone of their native Normandy. The pilaster strips of pre-Conquest architecture were replaced by broader, flat buttresses. They were still rather shallow and served little structural purpose. Blind arcading, with semicircular arches that sometimes intersected each other, became a popular form of wall decoration.

It was during this period that aisles became more common in Britain. Stately arcades of semicircular arches on massive round piers became a familiar sight in larger British churches. As well as round piers, the most common form by far, there were compound piers which were square or rectangular in section with thinner columns grafted on to the flat faces or cut into the corner angles. At the end of the period octagonal piers made their appearance. Piers were set on bases which were generally square and fairly plain: a simple roll moulding around the bottom of the pier, and perhaps a small leaf-shaped carving called an angle spur in each corner. The top of the pier ended in a capital. The cushion capital was shaped like a cube with the four lower corners rounded off like a plump cushion so that it was circular in section where it met the pier, and square above where it met the abacus, the square slab of stone that supported the arch. The cushion capital set the basic pattern for several main variations: the scallop capital, which had the rounded part cut with vertical fluting to give a scalloped effect; the trumpet-scallop capital whose scallops developed tube-like elongations; the water-leaf capital which had a broad leaf shape in shallow relief wrapped around each corner; and the volute capital which had leaf forms springing from around the neck of the capital and curling outwards, a debased form of the Roman Corinthian capital. The flat faces of the cushion capital presented the Norman sculptors with an opportunity that could not be resisted, and they are often vigorously carved with abstract patterns and figurative scenes.

Arches were almost invariably semicircular, the few exceptions being those that were 'stilted-up' into a horseshoe shape. Windows were still small and round headed, the wall around them often being cut back, or splayed, to maximise the light. Doorways became larger, but were still round headed. The semicircular arches of these features were now always

constructed of individual voussoirs. The roundness of doorways, windows and arches was emphasised by concentric recessed bands of stone moulding called orders. These were very often carved with geometric patterns, especially the chevron, a zigzag pattern that was well suited to the chopping action of the sculptor's axe. Besides the ubiquitous chevron, other popular mouldings were the billet, a sort of rectangular chequer-board; the cable, which was like a thick or twisted rope; and the spiky beakhead, a string of stylised heads of animals and birds often with ferocious beaks. In churches of this period the south doorway and the chancel arch were

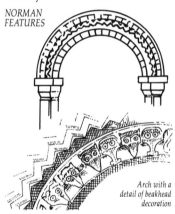

NORMAN FEATURES

Arch with a detail of beakhead decoration

singled out for special attention and several different mouldings were often combined to rich effect. Between the flat top of the door and the arch above, a semicircular panel of stone called the tympanum was often carved with an important religious scene. Christ in Majesty attended by symbols of the Four Evangelists was a popular choice. The tympanum was often the *tour de force* of the exterior.

TRANSITIONAL

As the name implies, the style of this period blends together features of the outgoing Romanesque style and those of the incoming Gothic style. Old semicircular arches sit side by side with new pointed ones. A common example of Transitional compromise is the 'modern' pointed arch retaining the 'old' chevron moulding. A distinctive feature of the period is the arcade of alternately round and octagonal piers. The round piers are of less massive dimensions than before. Octagonal piers had just made their appearance at the end of the Norman Romanesque period and were to become more common in Early Gothic buildings. The combination of larger windows and the greater height of pointed arches made interiors feel lighter and less severely monumental.

The newly introduced chisel was beginning to make its effect felt in a greater delicacy of decoration. Foliage capitals began to evolve. The chisel gave the masons the ability to undercut their designs so they could be more three-dimensional and eventually, in the mature Gothic style, more naturalistic.

EARLY GOTHIC (EARLY ENGLISH)

By the 13th century the pointed arch was the norm. Often they were quite acutely pointed as if the masons were revelling in the new fashion. The orders of the arches were simply treated with chamfers or roll mouldings to achieve a linear effect.

Piers continued to be octagonal and round in section, but there was also a distinctive innovation which typifies Early Gothic work and is easy to spot. Round piers were sometimes surrounded by four or more slender shafts tied back to the central pillar by rings of stone

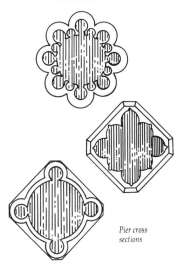

Pier cross sections

called <u>annulets</u>. These detached shafts were often made of Purbeck marble, the dark grey-green polished surface making an attractive contrast against the paler stonework. The bases of piers usually have two thick roll mouldings with a deep hollow between, known as a <u>water-holding moulding</u>. Capitals are moulded too. A single roll moulding where the capital meets the pier and, usually, a double roll where it meets the abacus give the appearance of an inverted bell, hence the name, <u>bell capital</u> or <u>moulded capital</u>. In the space between the roll mouldings the capital may be carved with decoration typical of the period, the most common being <u>stiff-leaf</u>, and <u>nailhead</u>. Stiff-leaf, as the name implies, is stylised foliage springing stiffly from the base of the capital and curling outwards at the top. Nailhead is made up of a string of low pyramids, reminiscent of the heads of hand-made nails.

There was a sense of restraint in the use of ornament. The decorative moulding most characteristic of Early Gothic work is called <u>dogtooth</u>, and was probably evolved from the earlier chevron. The rather unlikely name describes a string of open pyramids formed by leaning together four almond-shaped pieces, which must at sometime have reminded someone of canine incisors. A single order of dogtooth is quite likely to be found around the arches of windows and doors, occasionally arcades, and perhaps on a <u>string course</u> running horizontally along a wall.

The walls themselves were built much thinner. This meant that buttresses were now called upon to play a structural role, helping the walls to support the weight of roofs or vaults. To do this they were built out further at the base, and tapered towards the top, with a series of <u>set-offs</u> designed to throw off rain water. At corners, two buttresses were set at right angles. In grander churches, corner buttresses sometimes became major architectural features, polygonal in section and decorated with blind arcading.

The Early Gothic window has a very distinctive form: the <u>lancet</u>, so-called because it is tall, narrow and pointed. At the east end there may be two or three together, but they were treated as separate windows, each with its own arch and <u>dripstone</u> or <u>hood mould</u>. But by the middle of the century, masons had begun grouping lancets together in pairs and triplets under a single arch. In some churches as many as five or even seven were set together, stepped in height so that their points followed the curve of the arch above. The next stage was almost inevitable:

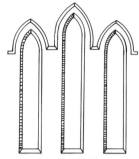

EARLY GOTHIC FEATURES

Grouped lancet windows

circular or lozenge-shaped openings were cut through the solid wall between the points of the lancets, and the very first stage in the development of window tracery, known as <u>plate tracery</u>, had been achieved.

HIGH GOTHIC (DECORATED)

Window tracery is one of the chief glories of Gothic architecture, and it was during the first half of the 14th century that tracery patterns were at their most vital and imaginative. The decorative focus of the church shifted from doorways and the chancel arch to its windows, a change of emphasis that was further encouraged by the increasing availability of stained glass. Plate tracery in the Early Gothic period had already anticipated the development of <u>bar tracery</u> in which a single large window opening is divided into <u>lights</u> by vertical stone bars called <u>mullions</u>. In the head of the window, the mullions branch out and produce intersecting patterns in stonework. Window tracery was made technically possible by the improved efficiency of buttresses which now assumed the main structural role in the building, enabling walls to be built even thinner and with larger windows.

Plate tracery was succeeded in the High Gothic period by <u>geometric tracery</u> which is just as its name suggests: the kind of pattern that could be simply drawn with set square and compasses. At its simplest geometric tracery might be a group of three circles. Another early form of bar tracery was <u>intersecting tracery</u>. Again the name is descriptive: each mullion branches out in two arcs, of the same radius as the window arch, and intersects its neighbour's branches.

Then masons made a discovery that was to liberate the rigid, set-square-and-compasses lines of tracery design. That discovery was the sinuous <u>ogee</u> curve, best described as a shallow S-shape. The repetition of the ogee curve wove a net-like pattern of tracery called <u>reticulated tracery</u>. Freedom of line was taken a stage further in <u>flowing</u> or <u>curvilinear tracery</u> which is the true epitome of the High Gothic style. An inventive variety of tracery patterns were evolved. In Europe, especially France, tracery developed into an even more extravagant style called <u>flamboyant</u>, from the flame (*flambe*) shape formed by staggered parallel ogee curves. In England there was no marked enthusiasm for this style, and soon the more regimented <u>rectilinear tracery</u> of the Late Gothic was to become the fashion. In Scotland, however, tracery

continued for a while to evolve more towards the French style. It was perhaps no coincidence that England was at war with France, while Scotland and France were allies.

High Gothic buttresses were not only more structurally effective, but more decorative too. Top loading with a <u>pinnacle</u> helped the buttress to sustain the outward thrust of the walls. With its elegantly tapering profile enriched with <u>crockets</u> and a foliated <u>finial</u>, the pinnacle also provided an ornamental finish. Crockets, nodules of stone carved like budding leaves, are found everywhere, making many features of High Gothic churches look as though they are about to burst into leaf. Buttresses often also had carved niches designed to hold figure sculpture. The corners of buildings were no longer supported by two buttresses at right angles, but by a single buttress set diagonally called a <u>French buttress</u>. Clerestorys began to get higher and sometimes needed support from <u>flying buttresses</u>, half arches that conducted the weight over an aisle roof and down to the wall buttresses.

Dogtooth moulding was replaced by strings of globular flower buds called <u>ball-flower</u>, and by <u>four-leafed flower</u>, four petals forming a square tablet. In the design of piers there was much more variety: a diamond-shaped section made up of clustered shafts was common. There was even more diversity in the appearance of capitals, the only common factor being the use of naturalistic forms. The overall impression of this period is one of organic growth and inventive imagination. It was a relatively short-lived style that was to give way to one characterised by a greater rationality and worldliness.

HIGH GOTHIC FEATURES

Geometric tracery

Curvilinear tracery

LATE GOTHIC (PERPENDICULAR)

The sinuous curves and convolutions of the High Gothic style were replaced by the right angles and straight lines of Late Gothic. The trend towards taller naves and towers, and larger windows continued. The chancel of Holy Trinity, Stratford-upon-Avon, has a greater area of glass than solid wall. Windows became so big that horizontal stone bars, called transoms, were needed to brace the mullions. Tracery was much simplified and tended to become upright panels with miniature foiled arches at their tops. Late Gothic windows impress not by the complexity of their tracery but by their sheer size and, where it survives, their stained glass. The Late Gothic style is characterised by a sense of verticality in all its features.

LATE GOTHIC FEATURES

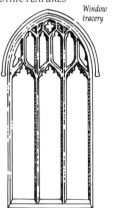

Window tracery

Doorways usually had four-centred arches, so-called because their curves had a smaller radius at the sides than in the centre, producing the rather flat-topped 'Tudor' arch. Above the doorway, hood moulds were now usually square, and the triangular spaces between the arch and the corners of the hood mould,

the spandrels, provided space for decorative carving which was often heraldic in design. Arcades, too, were frequently of four-centred arches. Their piers grew even more slender and were frequently octagonal, sometimes with slightly concave faces, or diamond shaped with shafts. Capitals were less significant and sometimes omitted altogether, the shafts of the piers flowing straight up into the mouldings of the arch. Foliage decoration virtually disappeared, apart from in the West Country. The four-leafed flower continued in use, but was shaped more squarely and set in a concave moulding. Buttresses were set in pairs at the corners of buildings, but unlike in the Early Gothic period they were set back slightly so that the corner projected between the two buttresses.

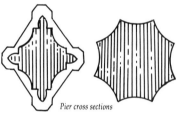

Pier cross sections

The Late Gothic style held sway for longer than both earlier Gothic styles put together. Few indeed are churches without some work from this period. It was a golden age for the carpenter too. Churches were furnished with wonderful roofs and screens, often ornately carved and richly painted. Stalls were provided for the choir and benches for the nave. The bench ends were often elaborately carved either with large foliated finials, called poppyheads, or with animals and figures. East Anglia and the south-west are particularly fortunate in their bench ends.

Throughout the Gothic period, the permanent fittings of the church reflected the changing styles of architecture in miniature. In the chancel the main fittings were the piscina and the sedilia carved from stone and set in the south wall. The piscina is a small sink through which the holy water used by the priest to wash his hands during Mass could drain away undefiled into sanctified ground. Its name literally means a little fish-pond, from *pisces*, the Latin word for fish. The sedilia are a row of recessed stone seats, usually three in number, that were occupied by the priest celebrating Mass, the deacon and the sub-deacon. Sedilia and piscina were often grouped together to form a single architectural composition. In the north wall of the chancel an Easter sepulchre occasionally survives. The consecrated Host was 'entombed' in this carved recess as part of the Easter celebration.

CLASSICAL AND GOTHIC REVIVALS

In the wake of the Renaissance and the English Reformation, the taste for Classicism returned. The first milestone was Inigo Jones's design for St Paul's in London's Covent Garden, a severely scholarly building based on drawings by the Italian architect, Palladio, for an early treatise on architecture by Vitruvius. Arches returned to their semicircular form. Windows became round headed again, and Gothic piers were replaced by columns of classical descent: from Greece, the Doric and Ionic, and from Rome, the Corinthian, the Tuscan and the Composite. The second milestone was the rebuilding of London's city churches after the Great Fire of 1666, when the work of Sir Christopher Wren and his followers firmly established Classical Revival architecture as the most fitting context for Anglican worship. With the 19th century came the return to Gothic styles which wrapped the final layer of history around most parish churches.

ABOUT THIS BOOK

The selection of churches that follows is by no means comprehensive: England alone is said to have 11,000 churches of architectural or historical interest. The churches in this book have been chosen in small local groups that either complement or contrast with each other. Although perhaps idiosyncratic, the selection covers the broad spectrum of historical church building and provides a basis from which to explore and appreciate the thousands of churches not included. It is a sad reflection on present times that most churches must now be kept locked. But the key is often close to hand either at the vicarage or rectory, or perhaps at a nearby cottage.

Finally, don't miss the misericords, my particular favourite. Not every church has them, but where they are found they are guaranteed to interest and amuse. The place to look is in the choir stalls. Tip up the seat, and underneath you may find a shallow bracket. This is a misericord. Its name comes from a Latin word, *misericors*, meaning 'compassionate'. Medieval services were very long and those taking part were obliged to stand for much of the time. The 'compassionate' misericord provided a ledge on which the occupant could perch while still giving the impression of standing. They were skilfully carved with a truly enormous range of subjects, sacred and profane, humorous and moralistic — all medieval human life is there!

THE WEST COUNTRY

Within St Lawrence's, Bradford on Avon

Detail from St Mary the Virgin, Fairford

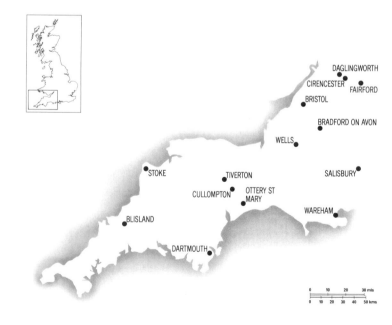

DAGLINGWORTH

CIRENCESTER FAIRFORD

BRISTOL

BRADFORD ON AVON

WELLS

STOKE

TIVERTON

SALISBURY

CULLOMPTON OTTERY ST MARY

BLISLAND

WAREHAM

DARTMOUTH

| 0 | 10 | 20 | | 30 mls |
| 0 | 10 | 20 | 30 | 40 | 50 kms |

BLISLAND, *Devon*
ST PROTUS AND ST HYACINTH
As you enter don't be alarmed by the south aisle arcade leaning outwards at what seems a perilous angle — it has stood that way for centuries and is unlikely to collapse during your visit! Perpendicular must surely be a misnomer here even though the piers and capitals conform to that Late Gothic style of architecture.

The church as a whole, however, is basically Norman, built on the familiar cruciform plan but with the tower in an unusual position: north of the north transept. The upper parts of the tower and the south aisle are additions of the 15th century. The south porch was built during the same century and from the same massive blocks of granite. Evidence of remodelling during the Early Gothic period is provided by the triplet of lancets which make up the east window of the church.

But the real charm of this church is the interior. Beneath its wagon roof, which runs the length of the building, quite disparate elements are brought into an evocative whole. Nothing could provide a greater contrast to the simple grey slate floors and plain whitewashed walls than the Rood loft, designed by F C Eden in 1896 and constructed by local craftsmen. Unashamedly exuberant, some might even say brash, its design is demonstrably Victorian. Yet it works, bringing to mind a taste of the colour and pattern that once enriched all medieval churches. Just as out of place, in theory, is the late 17th-century wine-glass pulpit, so-called because the base tapers to a narrow stem. Flowered swags, carved in the manner of Grinling Gibbons, hang down its corners and the whole is topped with a carved tester,

designed to act as a sounding board to beam the parson's voice down to the attentive congregation. Beyond the chancel screen, an altar of 1894 in the Italian fashion adds a further dash of colour, and yet another stylistic inconsistency, to an already eclectic interior. Though the academic purists might tut, here is an interior which manages to harmonise the diverse contributions of generations in the best tradition of our parish churches.

NEARBY
Altarnun, *St Nonna:* impressive Late Gothic church with one of Cornwall's tallest towers. Huge Norman font with faces and rosettes. Best of all, a set of 79 16th-century bench ends with an odd assortment of carved figures, signed by 'Robart Daye'.

Carved bench end at St Nonna's

St Neot, *St Anietus:* Late Gothic with High Gothic tower. Original wagon roof with angels and bosses. Unusual stone vault in south porch. Major collection of 15th- and 16th-century stained glass. Pre-Conquest cross shaft with complex interlace patterns in churchyard.

BRADFORD ON AVON, *Wiltshire*
ST LAWRENCE

No other church has survived such a chequered history. Founded about 700 by St Aldhelm, the first church here was apparently razed to the ground by Viking raiders. It was rebuilt by the end of the 10th century, but soon became too small for the growing community of the post-Conquest era and a bigger church, Holy Trinity, was built across the road. After serving as a charnel house for a while, St Lawrence was finally abandoned as a church.

Detail of a carved flying angel at St Lawrence's

By the 19th century the building was part private cottage, part schoolroom, and lost in a huddle of factory sheds leaning against its walls. Then, in 1856, the church was 'rediscovered' by a sharp-eyed amateur archaeologist who spotted the distinctive pre-Conquest Romanesque blind arcading on the upper walls of the former chancel. Surrounding buildings were demolished and the church emerged, surprisingly intact.

St Lawrence has a basic two-cell plan, but with porches north and south of the nave. Only the northern porch remains. Each porch was almost as big as the chancel, suggesting that they were used as chapels. Tall and narrow,

Bradford on Avon's ancient church looks its age

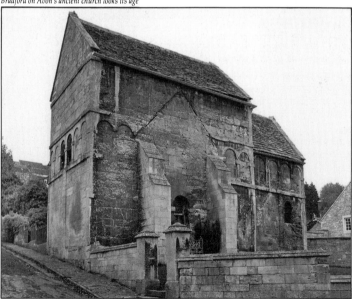

North porch and font at St Lawrence's, Bradford on Avon

the interior is lit only by two small round-headed windows. In the shadows high above the archway that glimpses into the chancel are relief carvings of two flying angels, carrying napkins to catch the drops of Christ's blood — all that is left of what must have been a remarkable Rood group. The altar and cross are constructed from fragments carved with interlace patterns, possibly from a shrine or altar.

What it lacks in size, this church makes up for in atmosphere. Primitive stonework shading upwards into darkness evokes an impression of simple devotion that lingers long after you step out, blinking, into the daylight.

NEARBY

Great Chalfield, *All Saints:* forms an architectural pair with the manor house. Mutilated wall paintings of life of St Catherine. Three-decker pulpit and communion rails, both of which are 17th century.

Westwood, *St Mary the Virgin:* remains of Norman tympanum carved with rose and lillies, emblems of the church's patron saint. Stately tower with domed turret. Late medieval stained glass, especially Crucifixion which can be seen in east window. Seventeenth-century pulpit and altar rails.

BRISTOL, *Avon*
ST MARY REDCLIFFE

'The fairest, goodliest and most famous parish church in England', so proclaimed Queen Elizabeth I when she visited in 1574 — and who dare argue? This magnificent church still deserves its royal epithet, despite the busy city ring-road which violates its space. Three factors conspire to impress: a cathedral-like plan, ambitious scale, and high-quality decoration with a touch of inventive originality.

Detail of the carving decorating St Mary Redcliffe's north porch

The north porch, St Mary Redcliffe

Inside, building styles can be found from the 13th to the 15th centuries, but the overall effect is Late Gothic. A comparison between the north aisle and the south, just a generation later, reveals the differences between High and Late Gothic work here. On the north wall of the nave, a corbel and other evidence suggest that the church had a stone vault as early as the 13th century — a rare luxury in a parish church. The wealthy merchants of Bristol evidently never spared expense in their attempts to demonstrate their piety — and excite the admiration of visiting ships.

It may have been international trade that provided the inspiration for the church's most interesting and innovative feature: a hexagonal north porch unlike any other in the country. Apart from its unique six-sided plan, the most striking part of the porch is its multi-cusped doorway with three wide bands of deeply carved ornament breaking around it like a wave. It gives a distinctly eastern impression. Islamic influence must be suspected, perhaps via Moorish Spain, but cannot be proved. The carving repays a detailed inspection: the forest of foliage gives shelter to birds and many other figures.

Above the porch is the muniment room (where the church documents were

The towering, cathedral-like interior of St Mary Redcliffe, Bristol

kept) whose neglected medieval parchments inspired Thomas Chatterton, the Gothik poet. His family had been church sextons here for almost two centuries. Beside the church stands a Victorian monument to this tragic boy poet who poisoned himself in 1770 at the age of 17.

While you are in Bristol, the cathedral and, across the green, the Lord Mayor's Chapel are other religious sites that should not be missed.

NEARBY

Yatton, *St Mary:* a High Gothic church in Late Gothic clothing. Unfinished spire. Highly decorated south porch. Wagon roof with carved angels and bosses. Monument to the church's chief patrons, Sir John Newton and his wife, known as Isobel of Cheddar.

Wrington, *All Saints:* tall, very attractive tower with fan vaulting inside. Turret for sanctus bell at east end of nave roof. Nineteenth-century busts of local 'celebrities': philosopher John Locke (died 1704) and religious writer Hannah More (died 1833).

CIRENCESTER, *Gloucestershire*
ST JOHN THE BAPTIST

Henry I founded a church here in the early 12th century, but the prosperity of the local wool trade and the secular interests of the abbey, which lay immediately to the north, ensured that the church was subject to frequent 'modernisation'. In 1399, the citizens of Cirencester captured and executed the rebellious Earls of Holland and Kent — an act of patriotism which earned them the gratitude of Henry IV who bestowed the deceased earls' assets on the town. With this handsome windfall the loyal parishioners built themselves a splendid new Late Gothic tower. Across the road, Black Jack Street takes its name from the blackened statue of St John the Baptist that once stood on the tower. The tower was meant to have been topped by a spire but its foundations did not live up to the masons' ambitions: the sinking tower was shored up by two huge buttresses and the spire was never built.

During the 14th century, chantry chapels were founded in the church by wealthy merchants with an eye on success in the next world as well as this one. The Garstang Chapel, built 1430—60 in the south aisle, has particularly good parclose screens with the family's coat of arms and merchant's mark worked into the carved decoration. The chapel of the Holy Trinity was set up by a consortium led by William Prelatte and Richard Dixton, members of the Weavers' Guild. Their brasses are still to be seen in the chapel, as is that of one of the chantry's priests, Ralph Parsons, whose richly embroidered blue velvet cope (ceremonial cloak) is still preserved in the south aisle.

The church acquired its most striking feature in 1499 when an ornate south porch, three storeys high, was built. Here the abbot conducted the extensive secular affairs of the abbey: it was, in effect, a medieval administrative office block. The largest porch in the country, it dominated the market place literally and figuratively too, since the abbey took a large slice of the profits of the weekly market — a frequent source of conflict between the clergy and laity.

The first part of the 16th century brought the last major rebuilding and produced the spacious very Late Gothic nave that is the heart of the church. Slender shafted piers, carrying flat Tudor arches, were built to a greater height than the old church. The number of different coats of arms held by the angels of their capitals reveal the many individuals contributing to this work of civic pride.

NEARBY

Elkstone, *St John:* Norman Romanesque with 13th-century additions and Late Gothic tower. Small east window richly carved with two rows of chevrons enclosing flowers. Tympanum of Christ in Majesty and symbols of the Evangelists; craftsmanship here is rustic but powerful.

The carved tympanum of St John's

North Cerney, *All Saints:* mostly work from around 1200 and the second half of the 15th century. Original medieval stone altar. Fourteenth-century processional cross. Graffiti of heraldic and mythical animals, and much else of interest.

Cirencester's St John the Baptist, dominated by its fine Late Gothic tower

The wagon roof and delightful interior at St Protus and St Hyacinth, Blisland

St Mary the Virgin, Fairford, is famous for its stained glass. The intimidating portrayal of Hell pulls no punches

The magnificent Rood screen at St Andrew's, Cullompton

CULLOMPTON/TIVERTON, *Devon*
ST ANDREW/ST PETER

The partnership of wealth and piety continues with a tale of two merchants: John Lane in Cullompton and in Tiverton, John Greenway. John Lane was a wealthy wool merchant who died in 1528. The Lane Aisle, named after its patron and built a couple of years before his death, is the outer of the two south aisles at St Andrew's, Cullompton. Its extravagance is conspicuous even from outside. Large Late Gothic windows stretch like webs between buttresses which are decoratively carved with ships and other emblems appropriate to the merchant and his trade: monograms, sheep shears, and the alchemical symbol for tin.

The other outstanding feature of the exterior is the tall west tower, built during the late 1540s from local red sandstone with freestone dressings. It is generously endowed with pinnacles and gargoyles, and the west face has figure carving including a Rood group.

Inside, a boarded wagon roof runs the full length of the building, there being no structural division between nave and chancel. Light from the windows of the clerestory, a rarity in Devon, picks out the gilding and colouring of its carved bosses and angels. Equally rich in its colouring is the Rood screen. Although the actual Rood is lost, the rocks and skull which made up its rather gruesome Golgotha base are still to be seen in the Lane Aisle. In a church that is already lavish enough, the Lane Aisle is marked out by that ultimate Late Gothic luxury, the fan vault. Corbels and pendants are carved with Instruments of Christ's Passion and John Lane's own emblems, familiar from the exterior. The merchant himself rests beneath a tomb slab disrespectfully robbed of its brass. But, lest anyone should forget his generous contributions to the church, an inscription on the aisle's west wall records his beneficence.

At Tiverton, the merchant-patron John Greenway was even less self-effacing. In a scene carved over the south door of St Peter's, the donor kneels with his wife before the Assumption of the Virgin, a convention more common in manuscript illumination. So that neither Virgin nor the earthly visitor should forget whose generosity and piety had enriched the church, his figure is identified by the initials of his name in Latin, *I G*. Brasses of the merchant and his wife are all that are left of their monument of 1529.

The Greenway Chapel at St Peter's

It was the south aisle, south chapel and south porch, all built in 1517, that benefited from Greenway's wealth. Ships decorate the buttresses of the south aisle, as at Cullompton, and delicately pierced battlements give its walls a lacy skyline. The porch has a stone vault with eagles, fishes and other motifs worked into its panelling, and is equally decorative outside.

In the same town, the fine Georgian Church of St George, built between 1714 and 1730, deserves a visit.

OHIO CHRISTIAN UNIVERSITY

DAGLINGWORTH, *Gloucestershire*
HOLY ROOD

An enthusiastic restoration of this small pre-Conquest church in the middle of the 19th century left little of the Saxon work undisturbed. The Victorian restorers did, however, reuse many fragments of the original masonry, and in doing so followed the tradition of generations of masons before them. When the west tower was added in the 15th century, the original west doorway had to be demolished but its masonry was incorporated into a new south porch. The 15th-century door still survives, and, above it, a pre-Conquest sundial. Even the Saxon builders had taken advantage of ready-cut stone according to the evidence of a window built into the north wall of the vestry: two narrow openings are pierced through a single block of stone bearing part of a dedication in Latin to the Mother Goddesses.

The Victorian restoration may have meant the regrettable loss of the pre-Conquest structure, but it also had a positive side: it uncovered the church's most precious possession, to which its dedication is a clue. When the stonework of the chancel arch was taken down, three pieces of Saxon sculpture were found set facing into the wall: carvings in high relief of Christ on the Cross (the Rood of the church's dedication), the Risen Christ giving the Benediction, and St Peter with the keys of Heaven. We can only speculate upon the reasons for burying these carvings face inwards — is a suppression of Saxon culture implied? Or had this style of sculpture had its day and become too old-fashioned?

Whatever the motive, the 'burial' of the figures ensured their survival with

Christ crucified, Holy Rood

much of the fine detail intact. The Crucified Christ has a particular dignity. His heroic figure dwarfs the Roman soldiers with their spear, scourge, sponge and jug of vinegar — this is not the sacrifice of a meek lamb, but a Saxon warrior about to triumph over death.

NEARBY

Baunton, *St Mary Magdalene:* originally Norman but with work of all periods. Nave windows illustrate three phases of Gothic tracery. Fifteenth-century embroidery. Wall painting of St Christopher carrying the infant Christ across a stream full of fish; in the background, detail includes churches, trees and a windmill.

Duntisbourne Rouse, *St Michael:* nave pre-Conquest, with herringbone masonry and 'long and short' work, windows later. Chancel arch and chancel, with crypt below, are all Norman. Some early 13th-century wall painting. Misericords. Saddleback tower in Late Gothic style.

DARTMOUTH, *Devon*
ST SAVIOUR

Built mostly in the second half of the 14th century, but with earlier and later work, this church has a lovely interior — but don't rush in. Pause for more than a moment in the south porch, of 1620, to admire the exuberant 14th-century ironwork of the door: its hinges extend across the full width of the door, forming two leopards *passant*, lean and hungry from the look of their prominent ribs! Their tails loop around a beautifully stylised sapling whose leaves and dangling roots form the background to the whole composition. The design is so fresh that it is easy to imagine the uprooted sapling held in the artist's hand. The date 1631 is thought to refer to a restoration.

St Saviour's magnificent decorative door

Inside, the 15th-century Rood screen survives more intact than usual. It shows some of its original colouring, has good tracery and particularly fine carving on its cornice. There are two parclose screens of comparable quality. In the chancel beyond, sedilia and a piscina with crocketted ogee canopies are grouped into a single composition. The stone pulpit is of the wine-glass type, though heavy carving and giant leaves threaten to overwhelm its elegant silhouette. At the other end of the church, a west gallery is reached by an 18th-century staircase. The gallery was built in 1633 but is carved in the late Tudor tradition. The gallery houses the Royal Arms and the Decalogue reredos that stood behind the altar in the years after the Reformation.

A very good brass of John Hawley, a medieval mayor of Dartmouth, and his two wives is preserved in the church — a fitting memorial to the man who financed much of the 14th-century building. There are also excellent brasses to be seen at the town's other church, St Petrock, which was completely rebuilt in the 17th century, but in Gothic style. It has a marvellous coastal setting, literally on the mouth of the River Dart.

NEARBY

Haberton, *St Andrew:* of the 14th and 15th centuries. Good tower. Norman font, splendidly decorated. Rood screen, panels repainted in 1870 with, according to tradition, portraits of local ladies. Fifteenth-century pulpit with later figures also worthy of note.

Kingsbridge, *St Edmund:* parclose screens with flamboyant High Gothic tracery. Thirteenth-century crossing tower and later spire. Monument by Flaxman to Francis Shutz Drury, 1817.

FAIRFORD, *Gloucestershire*
ST MARY THE VIRGIN

There is plenty in this lovely 15th-century church to engage the visitor: good Baroque tombs in the churchyard; imaginative sculpture along the string courses around the exterior; brasses of the founder, John Tame, his son Edmund and their wives; a lectern with chains and its original 12th-century feet; and much more. But above all else, Fairford is famous for its stained glass.

When St Mary's was completed at the turn of the 16th century, its high, wide windows were filled with specially commissioned glass, designed to link together stories from the Bible into a coherent expression of religious belief, starting with the Fall from Grace and ending with the Last Judgement. The team of glass-makers was led by Barnard Flower, who was born in Flanders but became master glass painter to Henry VII.

The unique survival of 28 virtually intact windows allows more than aesthetic appreciation: it gives us an insight into medieval ways of thinking. For example, it was believed that the events of the Old Testament foreshadowed those of the New. Therefore the 12 Prophets and the 12 Apostles were seen as counterparts and set opposite each other in the north and south windows of the nave. Each of the Apostles is given a line of the Creed. St James carries the words 'who was conceived of the Virgin Mary', while his opposite number Isaiah bears the text 'Behold a virgin shall conceive'. This pairing of subjects taken from both the Old and New Testaments was not unique to Fairford: it was a standard device which derived from popular religious books of the day.

The great west window presents a vivid scene of the Last Judgement. With a touch of inventive irony, Hell is portrayed as a glass-makers' factory where souls are wheeled in barrows to be ground in the mill and roast in the furnace: a subtle note of humour to leaven the dire circumstances of Doom. Elsewhere the humour is positively slapstick. The choir stalls have a very amusing set of misericords carved with the escapades of a busy housewife and her drunken husband, who ends up on the receiving end of domestic violence.

NEARBY

Cricklade, *St Sampson:* every period from pre-Conquest to 16th century represented here. Post-Reformation tower has good lierne vault with many bosses. Octagonal font is a typical Late Gothic piece.

St Sampson's Late Gothic font

Inglesham, *St John the Baptist:* small 13th-century church with contributions from later centuries. Wall paintings. Pre-Conquest carving of Virgin and Child of unusual design.

OTTERY ST MARY, *Devon*
ST MARY

Even from the outside you can tell this church is special. It has two towers raised above the north and south transepts, a rare arrangement said to have been modelled on Exeter Cathedral. The transepts have lancet windows and, together with their towers, probably belong to the church built here in the mid-13th century. The north tower has a stumpy spire which does nothing to alleviate the rather squat look of the exterior of the church.

Inside, the impression is anything but squat. Elegant piers of complicated section spring upwards to support stone vaults of exceptional quality and variety for a parish church. These are the product of rebuilding in the 14th century under the patronage of Bishop Grandisson of Exeter. Nave, aisles, chancel and Lady Chapel all belong to this period. The roof bosses of the Lady Chapel, carved with scenes from the life of the Virgin and other motifs, are worth detailed study. The furnishings too are mostly of the mid-14th century: the reredos, sedilia, parclose screens, choir stalls and misericords all carry the mark of Bishop Grandisson or his family. The richly canopied tombs of Otho de Grandisson and his wife are remarkable exercises in ogee and crocket — textbook High Gothic. Of great interest too is the gilded wooden eagle lectern in the Lady Chapel, one of the earliest surviving examples. The eagle balances on an orb which bears Bishop Grandisson's coat of arms.

Notable later additions are the 16th-century fan-vaulted Dorset aisle, the handsomely carved pulpit of 1722, and a font by William Butterfield who restored the church in 1850. The multi-

The eagle lectern at St Mary's

coloured marble font has a distinctly Byzantine feel and, though impressive in itself, sits rather uncomfortably in this otherwise 14th-century Gothic interior.

NEARBY

Ashton, *St John the Baptist:* 15th-century with contemporary heraldic glass, wall painting and woodwork: south door, wagon roofs, bench ends and screens. North parclose screen with especially fine painting of figures of prophets. Seventeenth-century pulpit. Altar rails. Wooden monument.

Kenton, *All Saints:* red sandstone. Late 14th century. Fifteenth-century pulpit. Rood screen of good woodwork, but inferior figure painting, with modern Rood loft. Good monuments.

SALISBURY, *Wiltshire*
ST THOMAS OF CANTERBURY

Of the original 13th-century church, only the chancel aisles and corbel table remain. The rest was rebuilt during the 15th century, the earliest part being the tower, built south of the nave and originally freestanding. Both nave and chancel have clerestorys. There are excellent wooden roofs in the nave and the south chapel — the latter built around 1450 at the expense of William Swayne whose name and merchant's mark are displayed amongst the angels on its beams.

An expansive Doom painting above the chancel arch presides over the whole interior. Its design was laid out in the early 16th century. At the top, Christ is enthroned on a double rainbow with saints at His feet. Behind Him, sun and moon shine on the Heavenly Jerusalem. At bottom left, the souls of the dead rise from their graves. Angels guide the

Part of the large Doom painting which can be seen at St Thomas of Canterbury

blessed upwards to Heaven, while the damned are herded into the monstrous jaws of Hell at bottom right. Though much later overpainting has no doubt coarsened the original work, we are still left with an unusually complete evocation of that vision of Judgement that at once thrilled and chastened the medieval congregation. More painting is to be found in the south chapel, but of poorer quality.

Also of interest are fragments of 14th- and 15th-century stained glass, an embroidered funeral pall, 17th-century monuments and a font which is probably contemporary with the 13th-century church, or perhaps dating from a little earlier.

NEARBY

Breamore, *St Mary:* major pre-Conquest church, 11th century. Defaced stone Rood over south door. 'Long and short' work. Old English inscription over archway to south transept, now vestry, reads 'Here the Covenant is manifested to thee'.

Farley, *All Saints:* built 1689—90. A fine Classical church on an equilateral cross plan with tower topped by urn pinnacles. Sir Christopher Wren may have had a hand in its design. Inside, the harmonious furnishings are all of a date with the church. The colourful 19th-century reredos strikes a solitary discordant note.

Wilton, *St Mary and St Nicholas:* expense was no object when the Rt Hon Sidney Herbert built this Romanesque-style church in 1841—5. Rose window, twisted columns and detached campanile season this Italian-flavoured concoction. In the chancel, black marble columns are the real thing, originating from a temple at Porto Venere.

STOKE, nr Hartland, *Devon*
ST NECTAN

The tallest tower in Devon looks out across the grey, heaving Atlantic. Late Gothic in style, it was built partly as a navigation landmark for passing ships. The impression of height carries through to the interior, thanks to the lofty tower arch and the airy spacing of the 14th-century nave arcades. The church is mostly of this period, with additions from the end of the following century.

The wide strides of the nave arcades lead the eye eastwards to one of the country's best Rood screens. Of 15th-century construction, it is decorated with shields and flowers between the unusually plentiful ribs that support the cornice, which has four bands of quite exceptionally rich carving. The wagon roofs are original too, partly open and

St Nectan's lofty tower overlooks the sea

The ornate Rood screen at St Nectan's

partly with a ceiling. The boarded parts are raised to the status of ceilures, with cross-ribbing in the north chapel and large painted stars in the nave. There is also woodwork of later centuries: bench ends of the 16th, pews of the 18th, and a parclose screen of the 19th.

The Norman font is an impressive square tub, which no doubt belonged to an earlier church on this site. All four sides have intersecting arches carried on blind arcading. Below the arcading, the bowl is scalloped in the manner of contemporary capitals, and the base has inverted arcading, like a reflection of the upper part.

NEARBY

Kilkhampton, *St James:* almost entirely rebuilt in 16th century. South doorway is a notable survivor of the earlier church: Norman Romanesque, chevron and beakhead decoration, good capitals. Nave arcade piers are each a single piece of granite. Bench ends are square headed, the usual fashion in the West Country, and carved with emblems of the Passion of Christ. Eighteenth-century organ. Monuments to the Grenville family, John Grenville being the rector responsible for the 16th-century rebuilding. Royal Arms and early 18th-century monuments by a local artist, Michael Chuke.

Launcells, *St Swithin:* enchanting site next to St Swithin's Holy Well. Over 60 bench ends carved with emblems of Christ's Passion. Other woodwork, 18th century. Capitals of nave arcade and 15th-century tiles in chancel both have *fleur-de-lis* motifs. Norman font with cable mouldings. Royal Arms, with strapwork, the work of Michael Chuke of Kilkhampton.

WAREHAM, *Dorset*
ST MARTIN

'Long and short' work at the eastern corners of the chancel announce that this is the work of pre-Conquest masons. Equally characteristic of the Saxon period is the chancel arch with its plain strip of stone moulding curving concentrically above the arch. In the 13th century the small Saxon church was enlarged and remodelled, starting with the north aisle. Here the piers of the arcade are typical of the Early Gothic period, each with four detached shafts of Purbeck marble from quarries on the neighbouring Isle of Purbeck. Like all medieval churches, the stonework here was painted from floor to roof, but only traces now remain: the ghost of a design with star motifs on the east wall of the nave, and some patterning on the east window, both 15th century in style. There are also fragmentary 12th-century wall paintings in the chancel.

A monument to an early 20th-century hero comes as a surprise, but a pleasant one. A recumbent figure, finely carved by Eric Kennington, makes a fitting memorial to the legendary Lawrence of Arabia, who spent the last years of his life nearby.

The effigy of T E Lawrence in St Martin's

St Mary's Church in the same town should also be visited, not so much for its architecture, which was savaged by clumsy rebuilding in the 19th century, as for a singular feature housed inside: a hexagonal lead font. The bowl has figures in high relief set beneath arcading. Although unique in Britain, it has French cousins in the Dordogne region, and is assumed to have been imported from France.

St Mary's lead font

NEARBY

Bere Regis, *St John the Baptist:* work of many periods, from Transitional pointed arches to very Late Gothic flat-topped windows. Roof of intriguing tie-beam construction with arch-braces, giving the impression of an East Anglian hammer-beam roof rather than the usual flat-pitched West Country variety. The beams have large bosses and are carved with figures. Web-like tracery spans the gaps between members. Norman font. Nineteenth-century stained glass by John Hardman and Co.

Wimborne Minster, *St Cuthburga:* patron saint founded a nunnery here in 705. Present building has Transitional nave with round piers and pointed arches. Crossing tower of late 12th century with interesting windows and intersecting blind arcading. Central and west towers. Early Gothic chancel. Medieval clock.

WELLS, *Somerset*
ST CUTHBERT

Late Gothic towers are the pride of Somerset, usually majestic in height and crowned with clustered pinnacles rising above delicately pierced parapets. Here is one of the county's best. For around a century St Cuthbert's had two towers: one over the crossing, belonging to the 13th-century church, and one at the west end, added in the 15th century. In 1561 the older tower collapsed, leaving the west tower to govern the exterior view unchallenged. An ingenious arrangement of pinnacles erupting in three stages from the buttresses produces a dynamic effect. The bell openings and west window are linked together by decorative panelling to form a unified composition with a strong vertical emphasis — a typical device of better-quality Late Gothic design.

There are other good examples of 'Somerset' towers at Chewton Mendip, Evercreech, Huish Episcopi, Isle Abbots, Kingston (St Mary), Leigh-on-Mendip and North Petherton.

Inside St Cuthbert's, 13th-century work is apparent in the piers, which are square in section with triple shafts in the corners, and in the plate tracery of the north porch. During the 15th-century rebuilding, the original piers were raised by almost 3m to support a clerestory and a magnificent tie-beam roof. The tie beams themselves are carved with small tablet flowers and have elegant fringes of tracery. In the centre of each is a shield-carrying angel with unfortunate wings that seem more like limp foliage than feathers!

There are shattered remains of two stone reredoses. That of the south transept represented the Tree of Jesse and was carved in 1470 by John Stowell. Mutilated survivors of the figures that once stood in niches among its foliage, many still with original colouring, provide a fragmentary image of what must have been a fine work of art.

The soaring Late Gothic tower at St Cuthbert's

NEARBY

Croscombe, *St Mary:* late medieval with wonderful Jacobean woodwork. Chancel screen with Royal Arms, pulpit with tester, reader's desk and pews, all of 1616, encased in strapwork and bristling with obelisks. Two fine 18th-century brass chandeliers complete the scene.

Glastonbury, *St John:* a complete 15th-century church. Exuberant tower shows stylistic affinities with Gloucester Cathedral. Two-storey south porch with lierne vault. Medieval vestment (piece of ceremonial clothing).

West Pennard, *St Nicholas:* Late Gothic tower with friezes of angels and star vault underneath. Timber and lead spire. More angels inside on richly carved wagon roofs.

SOUTH AND SOUTH-EAST ENGLAND

St Mary's, Uffington, a fine example of an Early Gothic cruciform church

The interior of London's St Stephen, Walbrook

BARFRESTON, *Kent*
ST NICHOLAS

Despite its comparatively small size, this is one of the most important Norman Romanesque churches in the country. As was often the case in the 12th century, the decorative focus of the building is its south doorway. Here the master mason has achieved an exceptional richness of carving. The tympanum shows Christ in Majesty set among meandering trails of foliage which embrace heads, angels and animals in near-perfect circles: a composition that could have leapt straight from the pages of a medieval illuminated manuscript.

The Norman doorway and tympanum, St Nicholas's

The arch above the tympanum carries three main orders, or bands, with figurative carving. Between each is a subsidiary order with purely geometric decoration. The inner order has foliage spiralling round a thick roll moulding. The next order is carved with a chain of medallions, each having a different subject. The medallion at the west end shows a goat being ridden by a monkey.

At the top of the arch is a seated bishop, perhaps St Nicholas, the patron saint of the church. The third main order has medallions bearing the Signs of the Zodiac and the Labours of the Months.

Before you go in, walk around to view the east end with its magnificent wheel window, a characteristic feature of the better class of Norman building, especially in France. The spokes of the 'wheel' are miniature columns and the rim is carved with foliage and winged beasts. Around the window are fragments of sculpture that originally represented the symbols of the Evangelists. Inside, the chancel arch received the mason's chief attention. Enthusiastic chevrons decorate both the arch and the shafts that support it. A blind arch on each side extends the composition across the width of the nave. Although the church had major structural restoration in the mid-19th century, the carved decoration was little interfered with, and what greets our eyes today is very much what was to be seen by those who worshipped here in the second half of the 12th century.

NEARBY

Upper Hardres, *St Peter and St Paul:* fragments of 13th- and 14th-century glass. Excellent brass (1405) of rector John Street, who kneels before a T-shaped bracket on which stand St Peter and St Paul, patron saints of the church.

Wingham, *St Mary the Virgin:* mostly of late 13th and 15th centuries. West tower of 14th century with small spire. Wooden arcade, whose pillars were dressed up in plaster overcoats as Doric columns during the 19th century. Rare 15th-century stone reredos with Adoration of Magi and Last Supper. Seventeenth-century monuments.

BROOKLAND, *Kent*
ST AUGUSTINE

Untouched by the heavy hand of the Victorian restorer who so often sought to return a church to its 'original' form, St Augustine's presents the kind of architectural *potpourri* that was typical of many parish churches. The earliest work here is the mid-13th-century chancel, with tall narrow lancet windows. But the church's claim to fame rests with two other features.

The first is unavoidable since it virtually obscures the exterior of the church: a huge detached bell tower some 20m high and 12m wide. It is completely timber built, a reminder that most early churches were constructed in wood. The internal supporting structure of four enormous vertical posts was probably built at the turn of the 13th century, but the distinctive shape seen today was acquired in the 15th century. At that time, the structure was clad in three tapering octagonal stages, giving it the overall appearance of a giant wooden Christmas tree. The 18th century added the finishing touch, topping the belfry with a weather vane in the shape of a flying duck.

St Augustine's has the country's finest lead font

The second distinctive feature of the church is its font — the finest of the country's 31 lead fonts. Small in size and cylindrical in form, it is decorated with two tiers of arcading. The upper arcade shelters the Signs of the Zodiac and the lower, the Labours of the Months. The naming of the months in Norman French hints at a Continental origin for this font which has no match in Britain.

NEARBY

Lydd, *All Saints:* mainly Early Gothic with High and Late Gothic windows. Some pre-Conquest masonry. Splendid tower, Late Gothic, built by Thomas Stanley, a master mason at Canterbury Cathedral. Double west door, an unusual feature. Many brasses, the earliest 1420 to John Motesfont, a priest.

New Romney, *St Nicholas:* one of the best in the Romney Marsh area. Large Norman church partly rebuilt in 14th century. Arcade of alternate round and octagonal piers. Windows provide textbook of the Transitional period.

Stone, *St Mary the Virgin:* an uncongenial setting and uninviting exterior conceal a perfect Early Gothic interior with all the hallmarks of the period. Thirteenth-century wall paintings of Virgin and Child, and Thomas à Becket.

DORCHESTER, *Oxfordshire*
ST PETER AND ST PAUL

The church is predominantly of the 14th century with parts both earlier and later: the north wall of the nave with round-headed windows is Norman, the west tower is a 17th-century rebuilding.

But it is the High Gothic work that shines out, especially the chancel which was enlarged in 1340. Of this date are the splendid sedilia and piscina, and the quite extraordinary window tracery. In the head of the east window is a flower-like design of six parts, set in a circle, the upper 'petals' reaching up like flames to the point of the arch. The design is not, however, restricted to the window head as is normal: instead a net of reticulated tracery spreads down to the sill, filling the whole window. And there is even more extravagant tracery work to come.

By a feat of ingenuity, the master mason has transformed the north chancel window into a Tree of Jesse. In the Bible, the prophet Jesse fell asleep and dreamed of the lineage of Christ as a great tree. This vision became a popular subject for medieval artists. Here, the sleeping Jesse is carved on the sill of the window, and the tracery sprouts leaves to become the branches of a tree rising from his navel.

There is much else to wonder at in this church: early stained glass; a lead font with Apostles seated under arcading, contemporary with the Norman church; a 17th-century embroidered cope; a wall painting of the Crucifixion from the 14th century, perhaps too enthusiastically restored; an impressive lych gate designed by William Butterfield; and a famous effigy of a knight about to draw his sword, dated to around 1280 and representing

an early but brief period of naturalism in sepulchral sculpture.

NEARBY

Drayton, *St Peter:* small, mostly High Gothic church housing a set of alabaster panels with superlative 15th-century carving in excellent condition, possibly fragments of a reredos. They depict episodes from the Life of Christ. The Adoration of the Magi is very beautiful.

One of the alabaster panels within St Peter's

Ewelme, *St Mary:* a perfect 15th-century setting of school and almshouses leads by a flight of stone steps up to the Late Gothic church with an earlier, 14th-century tower. The whole complex built by Alice, Duchess of Suffolk, Chaucer's granddaughter, whose bequest still finances the almshouses. Her tomb shows the duchess dressed in the robes of the Order of the Garter, but beneath is a second effigy: a chilling representation of her decaying cadaver.

DUNSTABLE, *Bedfordshire*
ST PETER

The church is in fact only a part of a large priory founded here by Henry I in 1131. The chancel and transepts of the Norman church and all the associated monastic buildings were destroyed after the Dissolution of the Monasteries: the nave was saved because it had been used by the townspeople as a parish church since the end of the 14th century. The nave is wide and quite austere. Divided into seven bays by huge piers and wall shafts, it gives a strong impression of the monumental grandeur that must have characterised the church when it was still complete.

The showpiece of the church today is the west front: an impressive, if rather

St Peter's displays a wealth of architectural detail from top to bottom

random, patchwork of mostly Early Gothic and Norman Romanesque work. Originally there were twin west towers, but in 1222 a storm brought both down in one night. The south corner of the front was given a hefty buttress in the 15th century and a new tower with a high octagonal stair turret was built at the north end.

Between these later additions stretches a richly textured façade of doorways, lancet windows and arcading, once arranged symmetrically about the round-headed Norman doorway. On the north side of this doorway is an Early Gothic doorway with a pointed arch, smaller but as rich in decoration as its companion. Over the doorway is an arcade of seven pointed arches. Above the string course, which runs the full width of the façade, there are two tiers of arcading on the left, and on the right, a pair of lancet windows rising the full height of the two-tier arcading. The sum total of these parts is an exterior of eccentric charm.

NEARBY

Eaton Bray, *St Mary:* a run-of-the-mill 15th-century exterior contains a 13th-century surprise — two Early Gothic arcades of exquisite quality. The south, of *circa* 1220, has octagonal piers and stiff-leaf capitals with generous leaves. The north, a decade or two later, has piers of eight shafts and capitals with even richer and more varied stiff-leaf. Thirteenth-century ironwork can be seen on south door.

Luton, *St Mary:* mostly Late Gothic with some earlier work. Walls with flint and stone chequer-board. Fourteenth-century font surrounded by freestanding stone canopy forming an octagonal baptistry, vaulted and rich with crockets.

GAYHURST, *Buckinghamshire*
ST PETER

This elegant little Classical church, built in the grounds of an Elizabethan mansion in 1728, is the very picture of gentility. The great house was first owned by Sir Everard Digby, who was hung for his part in the 1606 Guy Fawkes plot to blow up Parliament. At the start of the 17th century, it was acquired by George Wrighte who replaced the medieval church with this Classical gem.

The exterior is a model of proportion and unity: the windows are all set under matching semicircular arches with prominent keystones. The windowsills rest on aprons with stylised tassels, a nice detail. The doors are set centrally in the north and south walls of the nave under shallow porticos that rise to the full height of the building on Ionic columns. There is a west tower with shallow moulded pilasters clasping its corners. Below the bell openings, a blind hexagonal frame adds a slightly incongruous touch that livens up the formal composition.

Inside, we are in the early 18th century, frozen in its tracks like the figures on the monument which dominates the white plaster interior. Impressive in size, design and workmanship, the monument shows Sir Nathan Wrighte and his son Sir George. The work is said to be by Roubiliac, the Frenchman who was to become one of the finest sculptors of 18th-century England. Nothing is out of place here: box pews, two-decker pulpit with tester, column font, communion rails and Decalogue reredos together create a completely unspoiled interior. Though the architect is unknown, the influence of Christopher Wren cannot be missed.

The monument to Sir Nathan Wrighte and his son within St Peter's

Here the Baroque ambience and sophisticated charm of a Wren City of London church are perfectly at home, transplanted in the peace and quiet of the countryside.

NEARBY

Clifton Reynes, *St Mary:* 14th century with earlier and later work. Most notable for unique group of four oak effigies of *circa* 1300, two knights and their ladies, well preserved and of high artistic merit. The stone tomb of Sir John Reynes and his wife (later 14th century) is also of interest. The dog at Sir John's feet has a collar with the initials 'B O' suggesting that the animal was a real pet and not merely a heraldic device.

Felmersham, *St Mary:* model Early Gothic church built between about 1220 and 1235. Steps lead up to a west front with three stages of dignified arcading. Inside, the clustered piers of the tower arches are particularly impressive.

HOVE/BRIGHTON, *East Sussex*
ST ANDREW/ST BARTHOLOMEW

Two seaside churches, both built in the 19th century, but what a contrast! First Hove. In 1827, Sir Charles Barry, an architect famous for Gothic Revival buildings, turned his hand to a new style. St Andrew's, Waterloo Road, was the result, and the style is probably best described as Renaissance with Italian and French overtones.

The west front, facing on to the street, is divided simply into three bays by giant pilasters and topped by a square turret. This restrained, not to say dull, façade conceals a surprisingly attractive white and gold interior with Ionic columns. Stained glass in round windows adds a richer colour. In 1882, the chancel was remodelled by Barry's son, who added a domed ceiling with gold stars glimmering against a mysteriously dark background. First-class 1920s fittings by W H R Blacking add greatly to the appeal of the interior.

In Brighton, St Bartholomew's evokes a totally different atmosphere. Between 1872 and 1874 a local architect, Edmund Scott, created a vast brick barn, Gothic in spirit rather than archaeologically precise detail. Rising to a height of more than 41m, it is by far the tallest parish nave in the country. With no aisles or chancel, and totally devoid of carved decoration, the impact of the church is due almost entirely to its sheer scale.

Soaring recesses with pointed arches divide the north and south walls into bays and, in the half-light, give a rudimentary suggestion of nave aisles. The wall above each arch is punctured by a triplet of small lancet windows, and above them are the huge windows of the clerestory. Gaping through the east wall, a giant, plain, circular window rakes the nave walls with oblique light, throwing the subtle brick detailing into relief.

Within the cavernous interior glimmer jewels of the Arts and Crafts Movement: fittings of the highest quality made for the church by Henry Wilson in the years straddling the turn of the century. The metalwork is particularly attractive, especially the brass altar rails with inset enamelling, and the altar of the Lady Chapel which has a beaten silver frontal and an elegantly wrought cross. The marble font, pulpit, candelabrum and ciborium (stone canopy over the altar) are all Byzantine in style and perfectly suited to the stature of the church.

NEARBY

Glynde, *St Mary:* a neo-Palladian gem, built between 1763 and 1765. With its west portico and an east Venetian window set beneath a pediment, the

St Mary's is a neatly proportioned little church

church would grace any romantic classical landscape. The interior has the standard inventory of post-Reformation worship: box pews, west gallery, pulpit and communion rail, all of a date with the church. Unwelcome 19th-century glass marrs period feel.

The soaring, bare and cavernous interior at St Bartholomew's, Brighton

St Bartholomew's, Fingest, has an unconventional double saddleback roof
Inset: *The Tree of Jesse window at St Peter and St Paul, Dorchester (Oxfordshire)*

St Lawrence's, West Wycombe, rebuilt by the notorious Sir Francis Dashwood who used to dine within the huge ball which crowns the tower

The design of the west front at St Mary the Virgin, Iffley, has three distinct stages

IFFLEY, *Oxfordshire*
ST MARY THE VIRGIN
Built in the second half of the 12th century by the rich Norman-French family of St Remy, the church is of small scale and simple plan — nave, axial tower and chancel — but extremely lavish in its ornamentation.

From outside, the west front presents the most striking view. It rises in three clearly defined stages. At ground level, two blind arches flank the west doorway which is so deeply recessed that it occupies half the width of the front. Running around the doorway, without any capitals, are four continuous orders of chevrons and two of beakheads with particularly sharp-looking beaks. The design is completed by a semicircular dripstone carved with beaded medallions bearing symbols of the Evangelists and the Signs of the Zodiac. The middle stage has a large circular window with chevron moulding, a reconstruction of the 19th century based on sound archaeological evidence. The upper stage was mutilated in the 15th century when the pitch of the roof was made fashionably flat. The angle of the gable was lowered by slicing through the outer arches of an arcade which embraces three upper windows. This mutilation was corrected in the 19th century when the gable was rebuilt and the roof returned to its original pitch.

Inside, chevron moulding is to be seen everywhere. On tower and chancel arches it is coupled with an unusual flower motif. A capital in the south-west corner of the choir shows a bird guarding her nest, a touch of naturalism that contrasts strongly with the highly stylised decoration elsewhere, and anticipates the Gothic observation of natural form. The chancel was remodelled in the 13th century, and to this date belong the aumbry, piscina and sedilia. The black stone font is 12th century: a square bowl big enough for baptism by total immersion, supported on spiral shafts, the plain shaft being a 13th-century repair. In 1907, Sir Ninian Comper designed the tub-like pulpit that complements the interior.

NEARBY
Abingdon, *St Helen:* 13th-century church, but much rebuilt. Good spire. Fascinating nave roof painted as an enormous Tree of Jesse.

Nuneham Courtenay, *All Saints:* a domed temple with Ionic portico built in 1764 by James 'Athenian' Stuart. Designed as a 'feature' for the park which was being landscaped by Capability Brown. Severely Classical interior with inappropriately Baroque Italian fittings.

Oxford, *St Mary:* mostly Late Gothic. Fourteenth-century Congregation House which held the University library until

The south porch, St Mary's

1488. Extravagant south porch of 1637 by Nicholas Stone, with twisted columns probably inspired by Raphael's cartoons, acquired by Charles I in 1623.

LONDON

The Great Fire, which raged through London for four days and nights in 1666, destroyed most of the city's medieval churches. Among the few survivors, the Norman Church of St Bartholomew the Great in Smithfield has the most impressive interior. There are also medieval remains, mostly 15th century, in St Bartholomew the Less, the chapel of St Bartholomew's Hospital; St Giles, Cripplegate; St Ethelberga, Bishopsgate; St Helen, also Bishopsgate; and St Sepulchre, Newgate Street.

Disastrous though the Great Fire had been, it provided a unique opportunity for architects to build new churches in large numbers. The Act for the Rebuilding of London, passed the year after the fire, levied a tax on coal imported into the city to fund the building of 51 new churches. Some 30 years earlier, Inigo Jones had designed the country's first fully Classical church, St Paul's, Covent Garden. The rebuilding of the city churches established Classicism as the most fashionable and appropriate context for Anglican worship. It was not, however, the severe Classicism of St Paul's that characterised most of the new churches, but a more liberated and elaborate use of Classical design. An unprecedented invention of the new style was the Classical steeple: a Gothic structure dressed in Classical motifs. St Martin-in-the-Fields, built by James Gibbs in the 1720s, with its steeple fronted by a portico, must be the supreme example of the fusion of these two opposing traditions.

The hero of the day was undoubtedly Sir Christopher Wren, whose work set the ground rules for the new architecture. The cramped and awkwardly shaped sites that were the legacy of the Great Fire provided Wren with a challenge that he met with great variety and ingenuity. The best of Wren's steeples are probably St Mary-le-Bow in Cheapside, and St Bride's, Fleet Street; his best interior is surely St Stephen, Walbrook, with its magnificent dome, the first in any British church. Other Wren churches of note include

The domed interior, St Stephen, Walbrook

St Margaret, Lothbury; St Anne and St Agnes, Gresham Street; St Lawrence Jewry, also in Gresham Street; and St Benet's, Paul's Wharf. Wren's followers added a rather more theatrical element to the style he had established — 'fancy' was the word used by Nicholas Hawksmoor, whose masterpieces are Christchurch, Spitalfields and St Mary, Woolnoth.

In the 19th century London engulfed long-established villages as new suburbs were carved out of the countryside. As a result, Greater London has a mixture of adopted medieval churches and 19th-century churches built to meet the needs of the growing population. The medieval church of St Mary, Harrow-on-the-Hill, still holds its own, and among other survivors from this period are St Dunstan in Cranford, St Mary Magdalene in Newham, and St Mary in Northolt.

In 1818, an Act of Parliament granted a million pounds for new churches in the capital and the industrialised Midlands and North. The Commissioner's Churches, as they became known, were mostly of Classical design, leaning towards the Greek rather than the Roman which was now becoming outmoded. John Nash's All Souls, Langham Place, and St Pancras, Euston Road, by W and H W Inwood, are notable examples of this Greek Revival style of church architecture.

Greek Revivalism at St Pancras, Euston Road, built in the 19th century

As the century wore on, a reaction against 'pagan' Classicism set in as churchmen and architects came to believe that the only truly Christian style was Gothic, preferably Early Gothic at

that. Churches like William Butterfield's All Saints, St Margaret Street, and John Pearson's St Augustine, Kilburn, were built to embody this commitment to the Gothic ideal. But such purism could not last long, and by the turn of the 20th century a more eclectic spirit returned. There was even a brief vogue for the Italian Romanesque style, well illustrated by All Saints, Petersham, by John Kelly.

During World War II, many of London's churches were damaged or completely destroyed but, as the Great Fire had proved, disaster breeds new opportunity. Several modern churches are of interest, each varying in the debt owed to traditional values and design. At St James, Clapham Park, built in 1958, N F Cachemaille-Day used a pointed concrete framework which rises like the distant echo of a Gothic vault. On the other hand, St Mary Magdalene, Peckham, 1962, by Trollope and Colls, seems to defy tradition. In plan an equilateral cross, its four arms end in walls of plain glass that remove all barriers between the interior and the world outside, effectively denying what an earlier generation would have called the 'sacramentality' of the church. A good compromise is reached by St Paul's, Bow Common, where Robert Maguire and Keith Murray designed a building which, while reflecting modern liturgical taste — in the central placing of the altar, for example — still has resonances with the past. It has aisles and a second altar at the east end. There is also a subtle neo-Classicism in its use of pure geometry: a perfectly square plan lit by a central glass lantern whose roof of four squares recalls, intentionally or not, the gabled, pyramid-shaped roofs that once capped church towers a thousand years ago.

SHOREHAM-BY-SEA, *West Sussex*
ST MARY DE HAURA

Of the great church built during the 12th century at this small but thriving medieval seaport, only the eastern parts remain: transepts, central tower and chancel. The long chancel, with aisles, triforium and clerestory, betrays rare ambition in a church that has never been other than parochial — Norman churches on this scale are usually monastic in foundation. The nave was a casualty of the Civil War, and the surviving eastern bay was rebuilt as a porch in the early 18th century.

The 12th century was a time of architectural change: it started as Norman Romanesque and ended Early Gothic. At St Mary de Haura the transition between the two styles is frozen in time. From the outside, the tower hints at what is to come. It appears thoroughly Norman at first sight, with flat buttresses at the corners, and at the top, a simple corbel table with none of the fancy battlements and pinnacles that were to crown Gothic towers. But pointed arches, the fundamental Gothic innovation, have been introduced in the upper stage, and can be seen above the round arches of the bell openings.

Inside, the plain Norman tower arches look through into an eloquent exposition of the Transitional style unsurpassed in the country: the chancel of *circa* 1180. The north arcade piers are alternately round and octagonal. Two bands of stiff-leaf carving curl out of their capitals. The south arcade is a little later. Above the arcades is a triforium, a rare feature in parish churches, with both pointed and trefoiled arches. In the east end, windows are set in two rows of triplets, the lower group round headed,

the upper pointed. Triple wall shafts rise between the bays of the triforium and up through the clerestory stage to support the vault, which was built at the beginning of the 13th century in fully matured Early Gothic style: the transition is complete.

NEARBY

Old Shoreham, *St Nicholas:* Norman with some Saxon traces and 14th-century remodelling. Heavily restored in 1840 and 1854. Early 14th-century screen.

Sompting, *St Mary:* mostly 12th century but best known for its Saxon tower of *circa* 1000, with unique gabled pyramid-shaped roof, called a 'Rhenish helm', looking rather like an embryonic spire. Much of interest including Saxon carving of an abbot with his crozier (his ceremonial staff).

St Mary's unusual-looking tower is of Saxon origin

Steyning, *St Andrew:* spacious late Norman church with giant chancel arch and carved decoration of rare vitality.

SHOREWELL, *Isle of Wight*
ST PETER

The picturesque setting of thatched stone cottages is perfectly completed by the rather time-worn exterior of this large Late Gothic church with its west tower and set-back spire. Little remains of older work in the church: the south doorway is Early Gothic, and a blocked-up round-headed doorway together with a single lancet window suggest a date at the very end of the 12th century for the north chapel.

Poppyheads sprout from the old pews like mushrooms in the dim light of the interior. With the exception of the star vault under the tower, the architecture is competent rather than exciting. What is notable, however, is the 15th-century wall painting of St Christopher. The familiar river, across which the saint carries Christ, is enlivened by amusing fishes and

The animated wall painting within St Peter's

contemporary ships. On either side of the main figure are smaller illustrations of other stories from the saint's legend — an unusual elaboration of this standard subject.

The church still has its original stone pulpit, encumbered with a wooden tester in the 17th century. An hourglass of the same date serves as a reminder of the lengthy sermon that was once an inescapable Sunday duty. There are several good monuments to the Leigh family. That of John Leigh and his son, who died when only nine months old, shows the infant as a miniature adult, kneeling with his father. On a brass plate commemorating the two wives of Barnaby Leigh, the women hold his heart between them, obviously sharing his affections even in the after-life.

NEARBY

Arreton, *St George:* High Gothic tower, chancel and south chapel. Some geometric tracery. Doorway surviving from Saxon church. Good monuments.

Carisbrooke, *St Mary:* Norman nave with fine Transitional arcade of round piers and pointed arches separating Early Gothic south aisle. Chancel demolished in 16th century. Seventeenth-century pulpit and tester. Stately Late Gothic west tower rising in five stages.

Godshill, *St Lawrence:* set in a village famed for its beauty. Mostly of the 14th century. Airy interior divided into twin naves by Late Gothic arcade. Fascinating wall painting of Christ crucified on a living cross in full leaf recalls pagan mythology. Large painting of Daniel in the Lions' Den, attributed to Rubens. Sixteenth-century tomb effigy of John Leigh has his feet resting on two tiny monks who pray for his soul.

STANTON HARCOURT, *Oxfordshire*
ST MICHAEL

On a still day, the church reflected in the lake forms a perfect group with the neighbouring manor house — an image of the partnership of squire and parson that was the backbone of English village life for centuries.

There is still much evidence of the Norman church: north and south doorways, and round-headed windows in the nave and middle stage of the tower. But it is the Early Gothic work that catches the eye here, the result of rebuilding around 1250 when the church was dignified with transepts and the chancel enlarged. The Early Gothic keynote of the chancel is the stately triplet of very tall lancet windows in the east end. Inside, their verticality is emphasised by a framing of clustered shafts with stiff-leaf capitals. When the

Gothic: this is Early Gothic, from the middle of the 13th century, and complete with hinges, locks and bolts. It has trefoiled arches supported by turned shafts with shaft rings and moulded capitals. The solid lower part is randomly pierced with quatrefoil openings of various sizes. These were squints made so that children or kneeling adults could peep through into the chancel during Mass.

NEARBY

Burford, *St John the Baptist:* pleasingly eccentric plan, the result not of design but of continuous evolution during the whole medieval period. Impressive three-storey vaulted porch. Font is Norman, but its carving of the Crucifixion is 14th-century work, betrayed by cusped and crocketted arcading. Many monuments, and fine churchyard tombs.

A relaxed Alexander Fettiplace languishes within St Mary's

chancel was first built, lancets marched, or rather waltzed as they were set in triplets, in a stately rhythm round all of its walls. But some were lost when a Late Gothic chapel was built on the south side, for the use of the Harcourt family. The remaining south lancets have some of their original stained glass.

An uncommonly early wooden screen divides the chancel from the nave. Most chancel screens are Late

Swinbrook, *St Mary:* worth visiting for the 17th-century Fettiplace family monument alone. It fills almost the whole north wall of the chancel. Six effigies, in compartments arranged rather like boxes at a theatre, lounge on their elbows as they wait with a casual air of confident expectation for the curtain to rise on the Day of Judgement. Good tombs of 17th and 18th centuries can be seen in churchyard.

STOKE D'ABERNON, *Surrey*
ST MARY

The Saxon foundation of the church is confirmed by a pre-Conquest Romanesque doorway blocked up at the east end of the nave, and the use of Roman bricks in the masonry which were probably salvaged in the 9th or 10th century from a ruined villa nearby. Inside the chancel there is good 13th-century work, though a restoration of last century has given everything a rather scoured look.

Britain's oldest surviving brass, over 700 years of age, can be seen in St Mary's

The most important part of the church could easily be missed: set in the floor of the chancel is the earliest surviving brass in Britain. It commemorates Sir John d'Abernon, who died in 1277. From the excellent design and the craftsman's mastery of his material, we may infer that the art of making brasses must have been well established by this date. The figure is life size and his shield still has its inlay of blue enamel. He wears a suit of chain mail and a surcoat that parts to reveal *poleyns* (knee-plates) which are engraved with flowers.

Elegant 17th-century wrought-iron gates lead into the Late Gothic chapel built around 1490 by Sir John Norbury, a hero of the Battle of Bosworth Field. His helmet is preserved in the chapel. The occupants of the chapel were kept warm by a Tudor fireplace while they endured the long Sunday sermon. The seven-sided pulpit, with unusual carving, is Flemish but has an English backboard and tester grafted on. The church also houses a pair of ancient wooden chests, one from the 13th century with rather Islamic-looking star patterns. There are also interesting monuments, some painted, and fragments of good 15th- and 16th-century glass.

NEARBY
Chaldon, *St Peter and St Paul:* Norman and 14th century with a steeple of the 19th century. Famous for its striking and unique wall painting of the Ladder of Salvation — a huge, almost monochromatic composition painted *circa* 1170 and embracing so many subjects (the Seven Deadly Sins, the Harrowing of Hell, the Tree of Good and Evil, the Last Judgement, etc) that it is virtually a dictionary of medieval religious iconography. The church also has a rare 13th-century bell.

Ockham, *All Saints:* mostly 13th century. Famous east end of seven stepped lancet windows, framed by shafts with foliated capitals of inventive but harmonious variety. Wooden ceiling of 1530 with splendid bosses and some original painted pattern. Interesting collection of monuments and brasses.

TROTTON, West Sussex
ST GEORGE

Here is the oldest surviving brass to a woman: Lady Margaret Camoys, who died in 1310. Unfortunately, the rich canopy that once sheltered her life-size figure has been lost. A later brass, of 1419, is excellent both in preservation and design. It shows Thomas, Lord Camoys and his wife tenderly holding hands beneath an elaborate canopy with shields above. Lord Camoys, who fought at Agincourt, wears plate armour and the garter of the Order of the Garter strapped around his left knee. His wife wears the latest fashion in headgear and has a miniature figure of a child standing in the folds of her dress. It is a touching design, skilfully executed.

The oldest part of the church is the Early Gothic tower, which provides an appropriately austere prologue to the

The east face of the 12th-century marble font at All Saints

plain interior of around 1300. At this time we might expect to find the first stirrings of the restless decorative energy of the High Gothic period, but here there are none. For their date, the windows are conservative, not to say primitive: two lights with a quatrefoil opening above.

Perhaps because of the lack of a chancel arch, it is on the west wall that a painting of the Last Judgement is to be found. It is painted in red ochre and has been dated to around 1380. The standard scene of Heaven and Hell and the Weighing of Souls is flanked by two other subjects: the Man of the Spirit surrounded by the Seven Acts of Mercy, and the Man of the Flesh beset by the Seven Deadly Sins — pictorial reminders of how to get on the winning side come the Day of Judgement!

NEARBY

East Meon, All Saints: cruciform church tucked against hillside. Norman and Early Gothic. Best feature is the black Tournai marble font of *circa* 1135, with virile carving. Scenes from the story of Adam and Eve on two sides, and arcading with birds and beasts on the others. Tournai marble fonts can also be seen at Winchester Cathedral; Bourne, St Mary; and Southampton, St Michael.

South Harting, St Mary and St Gabriel: outside the church gate, the village stocks. Inside, good 18th-century tombstones. Church itself is High Gothic, but much rebuilt in 16th century. Roofs are Elizabethan, each part of the church having a different structural type: king post, tie beam and trussed rafter. Best 14th-century work in transepts. Square font and statue of Virgin Mary, both 13th century.

UFFINGTON, *Oxfordshire*
ST MARY

Nestling in the Berkshire downs at the foot of the famous White Horse Hill is this fine and very complete cruciform church, built in the Early Gothic style around the mid-13th century. The central tower has an octagonal stage which led originally to a spire. However, a storm in the 16th century brought the spire down, and an extra stage was added to the tower in its place.

Originally, the octagonal tower at St Mary's was topped with a spire

The church sets out to impress even before you go in: the vaulted south porch is of a size and elaboration that would not have disgraced a cathedral. Some figure carving survives in the point of the gable, but the statues that once filled the moulded niches of the buttresses have, inevitably, been lost. The shafts on both doorways have that familiar hallmark of the Early Gothic style: stiff-leaf capitals. The door itself is contemporary, and has good ironwork — the hinges literally snake out across its whole width.

On entering, a peculiarity strikes the eye. Over the north doorway is a large round window with six cusps of tracery. Could this be a clerestory that got no further? If so its windows would have been uncommonly big. The arches of the nave arcades, supported on piers of clustered shafts with standard moulded capitals, are unusually steeply pointed. Later generations resisted the temptation to update the Early Gothic windows so this church, unlike most of its date, has a good number of lancets set in pairs or triplets. Outside, there is a round recess for a consecration cross beneath each group of lancets: 11 out of the set of 12 survive.

Two 18th-century chandeliers are of intriguing design: a dove hovering over 12 branches which are shaped as serpents, with candles set in their mouths. This odd pairing of serpents and doves is found again in a font of the same period which can be seen at St Lawrence, West Wycombe.

NEARBY

Faringdon, *All Saints:* good work of all Gothic periods. The crossing arches of *circa* 1200 are the best part: each pier has 11 shafts and elegantly carved capitals, no two the same. South door has 13th-century iron scrollwork ending in dragons' heads. Monuments. Brasses.

Sparsholt, *Holy Cross:* mostly High Gothic. Piscina, sedilia and Easter sepulchre rich in cusped ogee arches. Rare 13th-century wooden screen with shafts with shaft rings, as at Stanton Harcourt (page 54). Earlier doorways with Early Gothic foliated capitals.

WEST WYCOMBE, *Buckinghamshire*
ST LAWRENCE

The hilltop site of the church is very ancient, going back to Neolithic times, but only the chancel and lower part of the tower are medieval. The rest was swept away in the 18th century when Sir Francis Dashwood, a man of notorious extravagance, rebuilt the church in the latest Classical fashion. The tower was heightened and topped with an enormous gold ball, so large that Sir Francis could dine in it accompanied by half a dozen of his fellow reprobates who were known as the Knights of St Francis of Wycombe.

The low chancel is 13th century, but disguised inside with fashionable 18th-century decor. Set in the ceiling is a painting of the Last Supper by Giovanni Borginis, whose father, also a painter, is buried in the churchyard. The font, also 18th century, is most unusual: a silver gilt bowl set on a slender wooden pedestal with three clawed feet, a serpent curling up the stem, and five doves perched on top. The apparently bizarre pairing of doves and serpent is

The font at St Lawrence's features the most intricate and exotic detail

not unique — the 18th-century chandeliers at Uffington provide another example. Their religious significance may be derived from St Matthew's Gospel in which Christ urges his disciples to be 'wise as serpents and harmless as doves'.

The showpiece of the church is the nave interior: a huge rectangular room with 16 giant Corinthian columns set around its walls. Heavy swags of stucco leaves and flowers hang between their capitals. Nicholas Revett, who was co-author of the *Antiquities of Athens*, the book that did more than any other to mould 18th-century Classical taste, had made designs for Dashwood's house and may have had a hand in the church too. The impressive ceiling, coffered and painted with a central gold star, was inspired by engravings from Wood's *The Ruins of Palmyra*, a book about an ancient city in the Syrian desert. The interior is a model of good taste and great erudition but, it must be admitted, little soul. Today it seems desolately large with the sad air of a faded ballroom after the party is over.

NEARBY

Bledlow, *Holy Trinity:* a Norman church remodelled in the 13th century, so the arcade of round piers with stiff-leaf capitals and pointed arches will come as no surprise. Early wall paintings of St Christopher, Adam and Eve. Fourteenth-century porch and some windows which display excellent High Gothic tracery.

Fingest, *St Bartholomew:* lovely village setting. Mainly 12th- and 13th-century church dwarfed by massive early Norman west tower with a most unusual double saddleback roof which is of post-medieval date.

WING, *Buckinghamshire*
ALL SAINTS

A short history lesson: when Britain was reconverted to Christianity at the start of the medieval period, it was a two-pronged attack. Missionaries came not only from Rome but also from Ireland, where the Celtic Church had been kept alive. Many differences had grown up between Roman and Celtic Christianity — they even had different dates for Easter. The Celtic Church built chancels with square ends; the Roman Church

The polygonal apse at All Saints survives from pre-Conquest times

had apses at the east end of their churches, the Continental fashion. Although the Celtic Church was defeated in most matters, the Celtic square-ended chancel triumphed, and when early churches were 'modernised' their apses were in almost all cases squared off.

The great importance of the pre-Conquest church at Wing is the survival of its polygonal apse. It has seven sides which are decorated with an arcade of thin, attenuated arches really little more than pilaster strips. Beneath the apse is a crypt which was literally unearthed last century. It has a central hexagonal space, vaulted and surrounded by an ambulatory. The nave is below the level of the chancel. Surprisingly for a Saxon church, it is very long and has aisles, which implies that this was obviously a building of some importance.

Many monuments are of interest, the finest being that of Sir Robert Dormer, who died in 1552, an edifice rich in Renaissance architectural motifs. A grim graffito scratched on the monument shows a man dangling from a gibbet. An amusing brass to a porter named Thomas Coates tells us that in 1648 he 'left his key, lodge, fire, friends and all, to have a room in heaven'.

NEARBY

Leighton Buzzard, *All Saints:* mostly Late Gothic, but boasting a splendid Early Gothic central tower with broach spire. Good woodwork, including eagle lectern and misericords. Fascinating graffiti on piers of crossing: a mason's layout for the geometric tracery of a window, and a 'cartoon' of a quarrelling husband and wife.

North Marston, *St Mary:* made famous in medieval times by its 13th-century rector, Sir John Schorne. He discovered a well whose waters cured eye infections and became hailed as an unofficial saint. His image appears on painted screens at Cawston Church, Norfolk and St Gregory's, Sudbury, Suffolk. Chained Bible, poor box and much else of interest to be seen.

Stewkley, *St Michael:* three-cell Norman church. Central tower with interlacing blind arcading and gargoyles. Showpiece is west front. Extensive but careful 19th-century restoration by G E Street who designed the pulpit, a neo-Norman cylindrical tub. Church also contains an interesting 15th-century alabaster of crowned Virgin attended by angels.

WALES

St Issui's beautiful Rood
screen, Partrishow

Carving at St Mary the Virgin, Haverfordwest

PENMON

GRESFORD

LLANFILO

HAVERFORDWEST

EWENNY

0   10   20   30 mls
0 10 20 30 40 50 kms

EWENNY, *Mid Glamorgan*
ST MICHAEL

The tone is set by the sturdy tower with its large, forbidding battlements. This fortress-like mass of stone, built between 1120 and 1300, is truly a church of conquerors: the Norman Romanesque style at its most dominating.

St Michael's has military as well as religious overtones

The oldest part is the nave and its north arcade of huge round piers, whose capitals make no more than a gesture towards decoration. The founding of a priory here in 1141 initiated a period of rebuilding to enlarge the church. The nave was heightened by a clerestory of deeply splayed windows, and the church made cruciform in plan by adding chancel, transepts and central tower. This part of the church is walled off from the nave and now has a separate entrance. Only ruins remain of the north transept, but the south has survived to testify to the awe-inspiring scale of the building. Three narrow, round-headed windows barely provide enough light to reveal high walls of monumental severity relieved only by bands of moulding and a few bays of arcaded triforium. Fragments of stonework casually litter the floor: a mass dial, a tomb slab with foliated cross, and much else of interest. The chancel, with its heavy barrel vaulting, is equally plain.

Its screen is 14th century, with linenfold panels inserted in the lower parts sometime in the 16th century.

NEARBY

Coity, *St Mary:* hidden from the road by the spiky ruins of Coity Castle. High Gothic style, large but without aisles. Cruciform plan, with a piscina in each transept. Sixteenth-century portable Easter sepulchre, made of wood and carved with emblems of the Passion. Among several interesting memorials, two diminutive stone effigies of 14th-century ladies.

Coychurch, *St Crallo:* built in the late 13th century when Early Gothic blended into High Gothic. Cinquefoil windows in south clerestory are an unusual feature. West window and dramatically splayed quatrefoils on either side have modern engraved glass by Frank Roper. Celtic cross, said to have marked the burial place of St Crallo. Stone with Celtic key pattern and interlace, bearing the ghost of an inscription.

One of St Crallo's beautiful windows

Llangan, *St Canna:* saints run in the family round here. St Canna was father to St Crallo to whom Coychurch is dedicated. Churchyard has the circular head of a 9th-century Celtic cross carved with the Crucifixion, and a 15th-century churchyard cross with its original head.

GRESFORD, *Clwyd*
ALL SAINTS

Set in a generous, round churchyard filled with old yew trees and with the village ranged around it, All Saints is a beautiful example of the Late Gothic style at its most self-confident. The church was completed in 1498. Its superb west tower rivals that of St Giles's in Wrexham, which is judged by many to be the finest in Wales. Great attention has been paid to detail: even minor elements, like the string courses, are designed as highly decorative features. In the 16th century, the tower was heightened and given its wonderfully original parapet on which there are standing figures alternating with pinnacles.

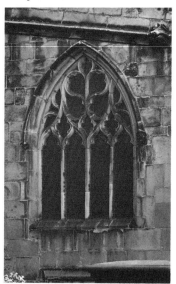

The west window of the south aisle at All Saints

Few churches boast such a complete 15th-century interior. Its woodwork is contemporary and of a unity and quality rarely found. The chancel screen has fan vaulting which supports well-carved cornices. The stalls in the choir have misericords with lively carvings and overhead is a good tie-beam roof with carved and painted angels and bosses. Exceptional stained glass, yet again contemporary with the church, is to be seen in the eastern windows. Even the octagonal font is of the same period. Such quality could only have been afforded under the patronage of a very wealthy benefactor. Here, the patron was not only rich, but royal: Margaret Beaufort, the mother of Henry VII. Is it possible that the king's masons, who were to start work on the stunning Henry VII Chapel at Westminster Abbey only five years later, could have had a hand in this building?

NEARBY

Holt, *St Chad:* red sandstone church with a 13th-century framework remodelled in 1500. South aisle bears the scars of musket shot from Civil War. Chancel crammed with all the fittings ordained as 'correct' by the Tractarian Movement. Heraldic font.

Marchwiel, *St Deiniol:* Classical with much 18th-century charm. West tower by James Wyatt. Stained glass with heraldic roundels, 1788.

Wrexham, *St Giles:* extremely impressive town church, rebuilt between 1472 and 1520, separated from the bustle of the streets by excellent 18th-century wrought-iron gates. As at Gresford, the patron was Margaret Beaufort, whose carved portrait may be found inside. Tower rises more than 40m and is loaded with decoration. In the 1920s a copy was built at Yale University. Much to see inside, including two memorials by Roubiliac, one very large, and a fine brass eagle lectern of 1524.

HAVERFORDWEST, *Dyfed*
ST MARY THE VIRGIN

From the highest point in the town, the church stares imposingly down the High Street. Traces of Norman masonry survive in the south wall, but they are of no architectural significance. This is predominantly an Early Gothic church with Late Gothic additions.

The decorative piers, St Mary the Virgin

Inside, the west end is raised on a short flight of steps. From here the view is purely Early Gothic, culminating in a great east window with plate tracery aspiring to the geometric. This three-light window with cinquefoil openings above illustrates very clearly the early stage in the development of window tracery that led from grouped lancets to fully evolved tracery. The Late Gothic nave windows are replacements set in during the 15th century when the clerestory was added. On the north side of the nave, an elegant Early Gothic arcade contributes much charm to the interior. From a distance, piers with clustered shafts and arches with five main orders of roll moulding, ripple in the side-light from the aisle windows. The shorter piers of the choir have detached shafts and annulet rings. Close to, the arcade reveals a wealth of vigorous carving in its capitals: stiff-leaf; animals; narrative scenes; faces. Many must be portraits of craftsmen and benefactors.

When the clerestory was added in the 15th century, the panelled tie-beam roof was installed. The supporting corbels on the south side are men's heads, while those on the north are women's — not sexual discrimination, but an echo of the old custom of separating the sexes in church, a tradition kept alive at Staunton Harold in Leicestershire (page 83). Also of interest is a late medieval mayor's pew. Its bench end, carved with rustic gusto, shows St Michael defeating the Devil in the shape of a dragon.

NEARBY

Carew Cheriton, *St John:* forms a bleakly imposing group with charnel house. Work from 13th to 15th centuries and later. Chancel floor has tiles, *circa* 1500, with heraldic ravens. Interesting monuments. Fine 11th-century Celtic cross a mile away at Carew.

Tenby, *St Mary:* set in the centre of the pretty hilltop town, high above the seashore, the church repays the care that has obviously been lavished upon it. Thirteenth-century and later, with much of interest. Aisles as wide as the nave. The 15th-century chancel roof has standing figures holding shields. Good monuments, among them one to William Risam, a 17th-century mayor of the town, which seems to have him kneeling in a fireplace.

LLANFILO, *Powys*
ST BILO

Approached through a lych gate, this little country church exudes a mellow charm, inside and out. The low exterior is richly textured with lichens and the occasional memorial tablet. At the west end is a short tower with a broach spire hung with slates — a carefully judged addition of the 19th century, and the last of many changes.

The original church was Norman, and the nave is still partly so. There are two lintel stones decorated with diaper patterns. Aisles were never built, so the church still has the simplicity of the Norman two-celled plan. The nave has a modest wagon roof, its panels painted white. The walls are also whitewashed,

Detail from the intricately carved Rood screen at St Bilo's

setting off perfectly the restrained natural colours of the flagstone floors and the magnificent wooden Rood screen which is the focus of the interior. It was constructed around 1500 and carefully restored by Nathaniel Hitch during the 1920s. Bands of rich carving embellish the cornice of the screen, leading the eye up to the parapet of the Rood loft, where new figures carved by Hitch are set in original panels of decoration. Above the parapet is the Rood itself, an agreeable replacement, again by Hitch.

A step down leads into the chancel which was rebuilt in the early 18th century and given a coved plaster ceiling. The altar rails are Jacobean. Also in the chancel is a 15th-century bell.

NEARBY

Llanelieu, *St Ellyw:* small 13th-century church, virtually unrestored. The Rood screen is deep enough to accommodate a loft that is virtually an upper room. At the back of it, a 14th-century wooden tympanum with some original painting of white roses on red background.

Llangasty Talyllyn, *St Gastayn:* richly furnished temple to Tractarian worship, designed by John Pearson, 1848, in a calm and contemplative lakeside setting.

Partrishow, *St Issui:* high in the Black Mountains, clinging to the hillside and saved in recent times from losing its grip, the little church has one of the most dramatic and remote settings in Wales. Contributions from all periods. Famous screen and loft, *circa* 1500. Two stone altars with consecration crosses. Font of pre-Conquest date with inscription in Latin naming its maker as *Menhir.* On the west wall a giant painted skeleton with spade and hourglass reminds us of the fate that awaits all men and women.

St Issui's, Partrishow, remote and ancient

One of the many monuments which can be seen within Bottesford's St Mary the Virgin

The stained glass window depicting St Catherine with her wheel at St Mary's, Deerhurst

St Bilo's, Llanfilo, still retains much of its original Norman simplicity

The beautiful stained glass in the east window of St Cybi's, Holyhead

PENMON, *Gwynedd*
ST SEIRIOL

The church is believed to have been founded in the 6th century as part of a 'clas' — a type of monastic community peculiar to Wales, which died out at the start of the 13th century. St Seiriol was the first leader of the community. Not far from the church, a holy well and what could be the remains of the saint's cell nestle beneath a low cliff.

Today the church is predominantly of the 12th century, Norman Romanesque at its most impressive in this part of the country. A low central tower is capped with a pyramidal roof of stone. Such tower roofs are rarely found in Britain, most having been replaced by Gothic parapets and spires. The south doorway has a tympanum with a boldly designed dragon, its impact tamed by eight centuries of weather blowing in from the Menai Straits. There is only one other Norman tympanum in Wales.

Inside, the nave is cold and darkly atmospheric: it is easy to imagine the monks intoning their plainsong at dawn. The chancel, rebuilt last century, seems insubstantial by comparison. The arches of the crossing are the most ornamented parts of the interior. They are carved with vigorous chevron, billet and other of the Normans' favourite mouldings. The base of a pre-Conquest stone cross has been modified to serve as a font. Two complete crosses, of around 1000, are housed in the nave.

NEARBY

Beaumaris, *St Mary and St Nicholas:* Fourteenth-century with additions of early 16th. Of later date, bench ends and misericords. Sarcophagus of Princess Joan, daughter of King John. Look out for interesting 15th-century alabaster tomb with effigies.

Holyhead, *St Cybi:* another 'clas' church of the 6th century, built on the site of a Roman fort. Some 13th-century work in chancel, but mostly a rebuilding of 1480—1520 with 16th-century additions. Fan vaulting in the south porch. Excellent Pre-Raphaelite stained glass, the work of Edward Burne-Jones and William Morris.

Llaneilian, *St Eilian:* 15th-century with 12th-century tower. Short passage leads from chancel to chapel of St Eilian with a fragment of a wooden shrine. Rood screen and loft with a painting of Death personified as a skeleton carrying a scythe. Many bits and pieces of interest include a pair of wooden dog-tongs used to remove canine interlopers.

St Seiriol's looks out across the Menai Straits to Snowdonia

CENTRAL ENGLAND AND EAST ANGLIA

Detail from St Mary and St David, Kilpeck

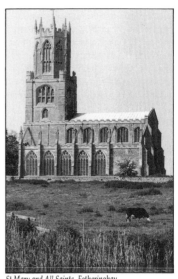

St Mary and All Saints, Fotheringhay

BOTTESFORD · BOSTON
MELBOURNE
CLEY NEXT THE SEA
RANWORTH
GREAT PACKINGTON · FOTHERINGHAY · WEST WALTON
EYE
SOUTHWOLD
WEOBLEY · GREAT WITLEY · BRIXWORTH
KILPECK · BREDON
LAVENHAM

0   10   20   30 mls
0 10 20 30 40 50 kms

BOSTON, *Lincolnshire*
ST BOTOLPH

As long as anyone can remember, the Late Gothic tower of St Botolph's has been known affectionately as the 'Boston Stump'. The name reflects its history and its appearance, but not its size. This stump is, in fact, an astonishing 83m tall. The body of the church is equally grand in scale, though it pre-dates the tower and is High Gothic in style. The port of Boston, facing the Continent, was a prosperous place in the Middle Ages. The building of the tower was partly financed by the Merchants of the Steelyard which was an English branch of the Hanseatic League, a prototype of our big multinational corporations. In the church is a black marble slab in memory of one of the Hanseatic merchants, Wissel Smalenberg, who died in 1340.

The 'Boston Stump', a conspicuous high point on the flat Lincolnshire landscape

The famous stump was built in three successive stages, which gives it a slightly disjointed look, rather like the pulled-out sections of a telescope. The lower storeys are the earliest work, of course, and though definitely Late Gothic, they still retain some elements of High Gothic design: an ogee arch over the west doorway, and ogee gables above the second-storey windows. This storey was finished with a decorated parapet and a spire was planned to follow, but did not materialise. Instead, at a later date, the tower was raised by another storey. But the townsfolk were still not satisfied, and a third programme of building topped the tower with an octagonal lantern, which may have served as a navigation beacon for ships entering the port. Inside, the first two storeys of the tower are completely open, affording a breathtaking view up to an intricate star vault, 42m overhead.

Not to be missed is an excellent set of 64 late 14th-century choir stalls, with Victorian canopies. They have fine misericords carved with a fascinating variety of subjects, among them a wolf preaching to a congregation of hens, a virgin and unicorn, a bear playing an organ and, appropriately enough, a mermaid luring sailors!

NEARBY

Bicker, *St Swithin:* Norman nave and clerestory on venturesome scale but, oddly, only two bays long. Early Gothic chancel with lancets and contemporary sedilia. High Gothic crossing. Fragments of pre-Conquest patterned stonework.

Wrangle, *St Mary and St Nicholas:* a marshland church with work of all Gothic periods, but predominantly Late Gothic. Well-preserved stained glass, datable to *circa* 1360, includes a beautiful Resurrection with sleeping soldiers in contemporary armour, and Christ stepping out of a tomb decorated with cinquefoil roundels.

BOTTESFORD, *Leicestershire*
ST MARY THE VIRGIN

The church's spire rises handsomely above the surrounding fields, but its real interest lies inside. An ordinary-looking nave leads to a chancel crammed so full with grandiose monuments that they literally had to raise the roof to fit them all in. The monuments are the tombs of the Manners family, who became the Dukes of Rutland.

The earliest is a small effigy, of 1285, representing Robert de Roos,

skull, a conventional symbol of early death. At her trial, the witch accused of causing their deaths called for bread, protesting that it would choke her if she were guilty — and it did! Among later tombs are two by Grinling Gibbons, those of the seventh and eighth earls, who pose rather pompously in Roman dress. There is also an excellent brass of Henry de Codynton, a priest wearing his Mass robes including a cope (a ceremonial cloak) which is decorated with the figures of eight saints.

The wealth of tombs and monuments within St Mary the Virgin

whose heart was buried here but 'whose body is buried at Kirkham', according to a later inscription. The tombs here provide a slice of history almost four centuries wide, reflecting the changing tastes of the aristocracy — both in costume and in piety. The tomb of the first earl, 1543, carved by Richard Parker, is the first to attempt lifelike portraiture. His wife, whose charming effigy lies beside his, must have outlived the earl because the inscription leaves a blank for the date of her death to be added later. The sixth earl's tomb includes a reference to his two children who were killed by 'wicked practice and sorcery'. A carving shows one of them carrying a

NEARBY

Grantham, *St Wulfram:* majestic spire of 14th century. Churchyard has two rare medieval gravestones with simple incised crosses. Impressive two-storey High Gothic porch.

Great Ponton, *Holy Cross:* west tower, 1519, richly crowned with tracery and pinnacles, and sporting a weather vane shaped like a violin.

Waltham on the Wolds, *St Mary Magdalene:* mostly very early 14th century, enlarged by George Gilbert Scott, 1850. Norman font, a foliated bowl supported by five round columns. High Gothic sedilia and piscina encrusted with heavy crockets.

BREDON, *Hereford and Worcester*
ST GILES
This is a fascinating church to visit for the way in which its architectural styles unfold very clearly the story of the church's development. Apart from the atypical choice of the north door as the main entrance, the pattern of evolution here must have been repeated countless times throughout the country.

A Norman Romanesque church was built here, around 1190, on the three-celled plan: nave, axial tower and chancel. To this standard plan, the north porch was added. Much survives from this period. The western part of the nave is all substantially Norman; only the west window is later. The north porch has a stone vault, a rare feature in a parish church of this date. Inside the church, a doorway above the entrance leads to a room above the porch, used perhaps as a treasury or library. Looking east, another survivor from the 12th century makes concessions towards the coming Gothic style: the west tower arch is Transitional, pointed but still with chevron moulding.

Fifty or so years later an aisle was added to the south of the nave. By now the period of transition was over, and this part of the church is a beautiful example of the Early Gothic style. Two pairs of lancet windows with trefoiled heads and detached Purbeck marble shafts are pure elegance.

Next came the chancel. The simplicity of the tracery in its north and south windows, which have fragments of their original glass, suggests a date at the very start of the High Gothic period early in the 14th century. The sedilia, piscina and Easter sepulchre are all contemporary. Set in the steps up to the altar is a good display of 14th-century

heraldic tiles representing some of the 'best' of English families. Belonging to the same period is a carved stone coffin lid of rare beauty showing Christ crucified on a cross of thorn branches.

Detail from the stone tomb slab at St Giles's

The north aisle came last. It has windows of High Gothic design but its short arcade is later, one of the few Late Gothic additions to the church.
NEARBY
Deerhurst, *St Mary:* pre-Conquest work of great interest. Herringbone masonry. Triangular-headed windows. Font, late 9th century. Among early 14th-century stained glass, a depiction of St Catherine with her wheel.
Tewkesbury, *St Mary the Virgin:* former 12th-century Benedictine Abbey on grand scale with radiating chapels in High Gothic style. Nave vault has excellent bosses with angels and scenes of the life of Christ — take binoculars!

BRIXWORTH, *Northamptonshire*
ALL SAINTS

A monastery was founded here in the 7th century, a time when Britain had only just crossed the threshold back into Christianity. The church of this date was built in the Continental fashion derived from the Roman basilica plan with the main entrance at the west end through a two-storey porch with a portico. The nave was high, with aisles and

All Saints' Saxon ancestry is well preserved

clerestory. It was separated from the chancel by a triple archway. At the east end of the chancel was a polygonal apse. This church was badly damaged when the monastery was destroyed by raiding Vikings.

The monastery was lost forever, but the church was rebuilt during the 10th century, and it stands today as the best of the country's Anglo-Saxon buildings, impressive both in size and completeness. From the older church, only the central nave survives, with its arcades set on rudimentary piers, little more than massive square piles of masonry. Around the arches of the arcades, windows and doorways are Roman tiles set radially in two rows, like improvised voussoirs. They are also used to mark out a string course around the building. Reset in the south porch is

a fragment of stone carving from around 800 showing the Eagle of St John the Evangelist in a highly stylised design.

During the rebuilding of the 10th century, the west door was abandoned as the main entrance and the porch built up into a west tower. A window, divided into three by turned baluster shafts, looks into the nave from the first-floor room. This is a common feature of very early churches — there is a similar window at Deerhurst (see previous page). In the 14th century a belfry stage was added to the tower and topped by a broach spire with pinnacles on its broaches. The following century the chancel was rebuilt with its east end squared off — a misfortune that was reversed in 1865 when the apse was reconstructed and the Anglo-Saxon dignity of the building restored.

NEARBY

Earls Barton, *All Saints:* the interest here is pre-Conquest too, mainly the massive unbuttressed tower. It has 'long and short' work, and a web-like surface

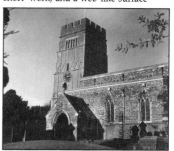

All Saints' powerful Saxon tower

pattern of pilaster strips. Windows are of good number and variety. The rest is mostly 12th century, with a 13th-century east end to the chancel.

Whiston, *St Mary:* on a quiet hillside off the beaten track. Unspoilt early 16th-century building inside and out.

CLEY NEXT THE SEA, *Norfolk*
ST MARGARET

The most striking feature here is the 14th-century clerestory which has five large round windows on each side with smaller two-light windows set between them. This alternation of windows is a pleasing example of the inventiveness that typified the comparatively short-lived High Gothic period. The aisle

focus is higher up, in the spandrels. There, immediately below the smaller windows of the clerestory, are ornate niches that once held sculpture. The figured brackets still survive, one of them a representation of St George and the Dragon.

There is good woodwork in the stalls, some with heraldic misericords, and in the poppyhead bench ends, one

St Margaret's, with its fine upper row of round and two-light windows

windows are, by contrast, Late Gothic, having tracery with a marked vertical emphasis under flat four-centred arches. The south transept, High Gothic in style, has been a ruin for at least four centuries, its crocketted gable, pinnacles and openwork making lacy silhouettes against the sky.

The west tower is plain and dumpy — such a rich nave deserved better. The south porch, however, does not let us down. The splendid two-storey edifice is Late Gothic, with delicately pierced battlements at the top, a frieze of shields at the bottom, and a fine vault inside. It shelters an earlier doorway whose free-flowing lines and graceful ogee hood mould carry the stamp of the High Gothic style. The hood mould stops are lions' heads, beautifully carved with flowing manes.

Though of the same period, the nave arcades, with their octagonal piers and simple moulded capitals, seem a little dull at first. But their decorative

of which represents a bug-eyed 'green man', that ubiquitous vegetation spirit. The font is carved with representations of the Seven Sacraments of the Church: baptism, marriage, ordination etc. A good set of monuments includes a brass of 1505 to John Symonds and his wife with a rueful inscription: 'now thus'.

NEARBY

Binham, *St Mary:* west front is the showpiece of this former abbey church. Early Gothic and Norman Romanesque work. Good stalls and bench ends. Chancel and abbey buildings demolished after Reformation.

Blakeney, *St Nicholas:* distinguished by its miniature beacon tower which looks out across marshes to the sea. Its big brother at the west end is Late Gothic, as is the nave. Chancel is Early Gothic with magnificent east window of seven stepped lancets, equalled only at Ockham in Surrey (page 55).

EYE, *Suffolk*
ST PETER AND ST PAUL
The main building material in East Anglia has always been flint. By nature, it is unprepossessing, and where the parish or the patron could afford it, church walls were faced with freestone from outside the region, often from the French quarries of Caen. But even the intractable flint was forced to succumb to the decorative urges of the Gothic masons. Flints were knapped (ie chipped with a hammer) to reveal the dark, shiny inside. Pieces of flint were then set into a design cut into a matrix of stone, rather like a mosaic. 'Flushwork' is the name given to this technique and it can be seen, *par excellence*, here at Eye.

Flushwork similar to this is used to good effect at St Peter and St Paul

The 15th-century tower is dressed from top to toe in flushwork finery.

There are friezes of shields along the base and above the west doorway. Among them are the arms of the de la Pole family, rich merchants who gained much political influence by lending money to the hard-up medieval monarchy. They were benefactors at a number of East Anglian churches. The two-storey south porch is also panelled with flushwork. Inside there is a 17th-century dole table (a stone ledge for distributing bread to the poor). An inner order of dogtooth moulding around the arch of the doorway identifies it as part of the previous 13th-century building.

After the richness of the exterior, the interior seems rather barren. The arcades have octagonal piers and plain moulded capitals and arches. There is a Rood screen, its loft and Rood restored in 1929 by Sir Ninian Comper.
NEARBY
Cotton, *St Andrew:* High Gothic. Splendid east window tracery. Sedilia and piscina under ogee arches. Good south doorway with foliage capitals. Clerestory and double hammer-beam roof, Late Gothic.
Gislingham, *St Mary:* both High and Late Gothic. North porch with shields in mouldings around entrance. Handsome font with emblems of Evangelists. Three-decker pulpit and box pews. Coronation of the Virgin among other fragments of medieval glass.
Thornham Parva, *St Mary:* thatched church housing one of the greatest treasures from the Gothic era — a set of painted wooden altar panels of superlative quality showing the Crucifixion flanked by eight saints. It was only rediscovered in 1927 and has been dated to *circa* 1300. A close similarity in style to paintings at Westminster Abbey suggests it may be the product of the royal workshops.

FOTHERINGHAY, *Northamptonshire*
ST MARY AND ALL SAINTS
A graceful church overlooking water
meadows beside the River Nene, it was
built all of a piece in the first half of the
15th century. Nearby are the earthworks
on which stood Fotheringhay Castle
where Mary Queen of Scots was
imprisoned for the last year before her

the corners of the tower. Beneath the
tower, a fine fan vault introduces a note
of richness into a light and airy interior
that otherwise has the stark atmosphere
found in many East Anglian churches.
At the other end of the nave is a pulpit
elegantly panelled with Late Gothic
tracery, and canopied with a rib-vaulted
tester with acorn pendants.

St Mary and All Saints is a fine Late Gothic church

execution. St Mary's was a collegiate
church, founded by Edmund
Plantagenet, a son of Edward III. The
prime function of such colleges of
priests was to pray for the souls of their
benefactor and his family. The church
was raised on an ambitious scale, but it
did not survive the Reformation intact:
the chancel was pulled down, and just
the nave and tower were left to serve
parish needs.

The nave is the epitome of Late
Gothic design. It is the work of the
master mason, William Norwood, whose
name is known by the chance survival of
a document of 1434. The windows of the
aisles and clerestory are so large that the
walls appear like screens of tracery
stretched between buttresses. The west
tower has a tall octagonal lantern,
perhaps inspired by Ely Cathedral. Its
form is echoed in octagonal turrets at

NEARBY
Castor, *St Kyneburgha:* 12th century with
much of interest. Noted for its richly
arcaded tower. Tympanum with
inscription commemorating consecration
in 1124. Wall painting of the life of St
Catherine and also fragment of 9th-
century sculpture.
Little Gidding, *St John:* Nicholas Ferrar
founded a religious community here in
1626 and rebuilt the church. Classical
west façade fronts a tiny, narrow, wood-
panelled interior full of charm. Late
15th-century brass eagle lectern with
ferocious claws. Brass font *circa* 1625.
Warmington, *St Mary:* all of one period
between about 1180 and 1280, thus
mainly Early Gothic. Good broach spire.
Rib-vaulted porches. Fourteenth-century
woodwork. Corbel in the chancel
personifies Wrath as a woman turning
her sword on herself.

GREAT PACKINGTON,
nr Meriden, *Warwickshire*
ST JAMES

At first you don't believe your eyes! Seen across the emphatically English park of Packington Hall, the four-square mass of St James's seems totally alien. Were it not for the gravestones dotted round about it, this monumentally severe building would hardly be recognisable as a church. The unique design is the result of a collaboration between the fourth Earl of Aylesford and the Italian architect, Joseph Bonomi. The earl was a keen student of Roman architecture, and features of the church seem to have been inspired directly by Roman ruins.

The building was completed in 1790. In plan, it is square with an inset equilateral cross, an internal division that is ingeniously articulated by the exterior: over the corner squares there are short towers with shallow domes; at the ends of the arms of the cross, semicircular windows divided into three parts are set high in the blank brick walls beneath broken pediments. These lunettes are most probably derived from the windows of the Diocletian Baths in Rome. A drawing of the interior of this ancient building survives in the Earl of Aylesford's library, and shows clear affinities with the church. It may also have suggested the cavernous groined

St James's has a striking, almost secular appearance

The interior of St James's seems starkly functional when compared with most churches

vault that broods over the central space. The arms of the cross have short tunnel vaults with simple coffering. The central vault is carried, visually but not structurally, on four Doric columns — not the normal tall and slender variety, but thick, sturdy and bulging outwards as though they were being squashed down by the weight of the vault.

The overall effect is nobly primitive: an interior that appeals more to the cool intellect than to the warm emotion. In a setting of such gravity, the altar painting of angels worshipping the Sacred Monogram, by Rigaud, seems inaptly lightweight.

NEARBY

Berkeswell, *St John the Baptist:* Norman village church. Crypt beneath chancel. Two-storey timber porch. South gallery.

Knowle, *St John, St Lawrence and St Anne:* Late Gothic on ambitious scale. South transept roof with good bosses. Pulpit with hourglass. Foliated misericords. Two sets of sedilia and piscina of different periods.

Warwick, *St Mary:* Late Gothic Beauchamp Chapel is deservedly famous for lavish decoration bordering on ostentation. Large 12th-century crypt. Rest of church destroyed by fire in 17th century and rebuilt *circa* 1700. Packed with interest.

GREAT WITLEY,
Hereford and Worcester
ST MICHAEL

St Michael's stands beside the gaunt ruin of Witley Court, home of the Foley family. The church was built, in 1735, by the widow of the first Lord Foley, to fulfil the plans of her late husband. Its architect is not documented, but circumstances suggest James Gibbs. The portico at the west end has two Tuscan columns supporting a pediment with a bell turret and cupola above — a neat example of the grammar of Classical design that had been invented for the new City of London churches by Wren and his followers.

A hint of Italy hangs about the exterior, but hardly enough to prepare the visitor for the surprise inside: a white and gold interior, the ceiling set with painted panels, the walls alive with Baroque ornamentation verging on the Rococo. This is a scene that might have been transported from the Continent to the grey English countryside, an observation that is almost literally true.

Alas, the Duke's son gambled away the family fortune and a generation after it was completed, Canons Park was taken apart and sold off piecemeal. Only the estate church, St Lawrence at Little Stanmore, remains intact.

The second Lord Foley picked up three big paintings by Antonio Bellucci (a Nativity, a Deposition and an Ascension) and 20 smaller ones. He also bought ten stained-glass windows, made by Joshua Price to designs by Francisco Sleter. Moulds were taken of the stucco work at Canons Park and it was reproduced in papier-mâché. All these spoils were taken to Great Witley and fitted together so skilfully that they look tailor-made for the church. As the first Lord Foley looks down from the theatrical tableau of his Classical marble monument, he must feel proud of his son's initiative — not such a complimentary sentiment that the first Duke of Chandos is likely to share.

St Michael's sumptuous interior

For the second surprise is that the decor here is hand-me-down finery acquired second-hand from Canons Park in north London. The first Duke of Chandos had built a great house there, employing French and Italian artists and craftsmen to decorate it with such extravagance that it was notorious in its own day.

NEARBY
Martley, *St Peter:* work from 12th to 15th centuries. Large red Late Gothic tower. Notable 13th-century painted wall decoration in chancel and 15th-century scenes of St Martin and the Beggar, and the Adoration of the Magi. Alabaster effigy of a knight, *circa* 1460.

KILPECK, *Hereford and Worcester*
ST MARY AND ST DAVID
This truly remarkable little church, built towards the middle of the 12th century, is exceptional on two counts: the intact survival of its Norman three-celled plan of nave, chancel and apse, with virtually no later alterations; and a profusion of lively carved decoration, which has been preserved in sharp detail by the hard red sandstone. At the west end, stylised dragons' jaws jutting out of the pilaster tops reveal a quite startling Viking influence, as though they had been hacked off the prow of a raider's ship. Beneath the eaves, a corbel table runs all the way round the church. It has 74 figuratively carved corbels, probably the work of more than one craftsman. The most eastern point of the chancel was always of particular significance, and here the corbel is carved as a Lamb with the Cross, the Agnus Dei.

The magnificently carved doorway at St Mary and St David

The carved corbels act as a prologue to the more sophisticated work of the south doorway, whose jambs writhe with decoration. Long, convoluted dragons climb up one side and down the other. On the left, two warriors with pointed caps are entangled in the coils of a trailing vine which binds them, in combat perhaps, to the dragon. On the capital above is a salamander, symbol of the power of safe passage through evil. The capital on the right-hand side is a 'green man', a pagan vegetation spirit symbolising resurrection through sacrifice. The imagery of the capitals leads directly to that of the tympanum which is carved with a Tree of Life.

As usual, the chancel arch is the decorative focus of the interior. Each of its shafts is a column of three Apostles, standing one above the other. The design is probably derived from a Continental model. The formal, rather stiff style of carving contrasts with the figures of the doorway, and suggests the hand of yet another mason. Kilpeck presents a fusion of several different artistic influences: Viking, Celtic and Continental. Its carving is an endlessly fascinating reflection of the cultural melting-pot of 12th-century Britain.

NEARBY
Bacton, *St Faith:* 17th-century frontal with rich embroidery. Tomb of Blanche Parry, maid-of-honour to Elizabeth I. She kneels before the Virgin Queen with almost religious devotion. 'A maid in court and never no man's wife, with the maiden queen a maid did end my life', boasts the verbose inscription.
Rowlestone, *St Peter:* 12th century. South doorway and chancel arch carved beautifully with many birds. Excellent tympanum of Christ in Majesty.

LAVENHAM, *Suffolk*
ST PETER AND ST PAUL

Wool merchants were the oil barons of the later Middle Ages. The centres of production in East Anglia and the West Country became boom towns, their wealth reflected in the extravagant 'wool churches' raised by the merchants, almost always in the Late Gothic style. The benefactors here were the merchant families of Springe and Branch, and the Earls of Oxford who owned the manor of Lavenham.

All is Late Gothic, except the chancel and a miniature spire for the sanctus bell at the east end of nave, which are earlier, High Gothic work. The tower is built of knapped flints (see Eye, page 76), used to good decorative effect around the windows and elsewhere. Its base has the merchant's mark of the Springe family and the arms of the Earls of Oxford, as well as emblems of the patron saints of the church: crossed keys for Peter and swords for Paul. The sturdy buttresses have many set-offs

Great wealth poured into the 'wool church' of St Peter and St Paul

which seem to impel the tower ever upwards with a relentless self-confidence. But it comes to an abrupt end, with neither the presence of pinnacles nor battlements to soften the church's skyline.

The south porch is fan vaulted and has heraldic references to the Earls of Oxford, whose badge was a boar. The nave arcades have battlemented capitals. On the walls, blank panelling brings all the architectural elements into a unified composition. North and south chapels have inscriptions recording Thomas Branch and Thomas Springe as their respective donors.

For all their extravagance, or perhaps because of it, the well-heeled Late Gothic wool churches often seem to lack the imagination and spirituality of earlier Gothic periods: an impression confirmed at Lavenham by a degree of regimentation in design, and by the worldly repetition of family emblems and donors' inscriptions which remind us that these rich merchants saw their benefactions to the Church as a sound business proposition, an investment in the life hereafter. Our faith is a little restored by the brass of Allaine Dister, 1534, which records his bequest of a 'yearly rent, which shall be every Whitsuntide, among the poorest spent'.

NEARBY

Long Melford, *Holy Trinity:* sumptuous Late Gothic with much of interest. Lady Chapel. Chantry with fan-vaulted room for priest and fireplace. Fifteenth-century stained glass. Brasses. Tombs.

Stoke-by-Nayland, *St Mary:* stately tower of 15th century, particularly ornate. South door with tracery and tiny figures forming a schematic Tree of Jesse. Many interesting brasses and monuments to be seen.

MELBOURNE, *Derbyshire*
ST MICHAEL AND ST MARY

This is a large and, among Norman parish churches, a singularly ambitious building: cruciform in plan with twin west towers and a crossing tower. Both transepts and chancel originally had semicircular apses. The chancel had an upper storey — a very rare feature. This has left its mark on the east wall of the central tower, where the sloping lines of the lost roof are clearly seen. Archaeological details like these are, in fact, the chief interest of the exterior since nearby buildings preclude good views of the church.

The interior cannot fail to impress. To begin with there is a narthex, formed by the two vaulted square spaces beneath the west towers with a rectangular vault stretched between them. This in turn supports a west gallery opening into the nave, a Continental arrangement unknown elsewhere in Britain. The thick round piers of the arcades march down the nave at a brisk pace, so closely spaced that their heavily chevroned arches had to be stilted up in order to achieve a decent height.

Above the arcades, the clerestory has a walkway. On the north side, the windows are round headed and the wall passage opens into the nave through a triple arch in front of each window. The south clerestory is a 13th-century variation on the same theme: its windows being pointed and set in pairs behind twin pointed arches. Most of the building appears to date from the 12th century. But why a church of this stature in such an apparently insignificant place? The village lay in the diocese of Carlisle, newly founded in 1133. The first bishop, Adelulf, found Carlisle

Sturdy Norman architecture within St Michael and St Mary

uncomfortably close to the untamed Scottish border. Preferring the safer southern part of the diocese, he established a second residence for himself at Melbourne and rebuilt the church on a scale befitting that of an unofficial cathedral.

NEARBY

Breedon on the Hill, *St Mary:* dramatic setting. Fabulous collection of Saxon sculpture, perhaps 8th century. Jacobean family pew with elaborate decoration.

Staunton Harold, *Holy Trinity:* built in Gothic style during the Commonwealth, a rare achievement, by Sir Richard Shirley, a royalist 'whose singular praise it is to have done the best in the worst times', says the inscription over the west door. For his pains, Sir Richard died in the Tower, in 1656.

RANWORTH, *Norfolk*
ST HELEN

East Anglia is unusually fortunate in the number and quality of its surviving painted Rood screens: here at Ranworth is the best of them. Apart from the loss of the Rood loft parapet, the screen stands today just as it did when it was constructed in the first part of the 15th century. It stretches the full width of the church and is divided into three parts. The central section has three openings on either side of the chancel entrance. The mullions between them fan out at

headed Dragon of Evil, is one of the finest paintings.

Forming a 15th-century ensemble with the screen is a cantor's desk which must originally have stood in the Rood loft. Designed like a simple reading desk, it is painted with a page of plainsong on one side and the Eagle of St John on the other. As if this survival were not remarkable enough, the church's *Sarum Antiphoner*, an exquisitely illuminated manuscript that first rested on that very cantor's desk four centuries ago, was restored to the church in 1912.

The skills of the woodcarver and the artist can be seen within St Helen's

the top into a ribbed vault which supports the carved cornice. All is richly painted with geometric designs. Beneath each opening is a pair of panels with painted saints, 12 in all, a work of the highest quality.

Minute attention is paid to detail: the tiny flowers and birds are identifiable as local marshland flora and fauna. To the left and right, partition walls screen off separate areas for side altars. They have brackets for candles, supported by ogee-shaped flying buttresses decorated with crockets. The screen behind the altars is not pierced; instead painted panels, framed by mullions and tracery, act as reredoses. The partition walls have figures too: the Archangel Michael, wielding a sword above his head and trampling on the six-

NEARBY

Barton Turf, *St Michael and All Angels:* all angels it certainly is on the mid-15th-century screen painted with the Nine Orders of the angelic hierarchy. Late Gothic architecture. Poppyheads.

Ludham, *St Catherine:* late 15th-century screen with kings and saints. Wooden tympanum in chancel arch painted with Crucifixion. After the Reformation it was turned around and the back painted with the Royal Arms of Elizabeth I. Now restored to its original orientation.

Worstead, *St Mary:* built in the second half of the 14th century but still retaining some High Gothic ornament. Excellent tower. Painted Rood screen. Tower screen and gallery.

The painted Rood screen at St Helen's, Ranworth, is the church's greatest glory

The fabric of St Giles's, Bredon, faithfully reflects the evolution of medieval church architecture

One of the magnificent painted altar panels depicting the Crucifixion at St Mary's, Thornham Parva

Detail from the Doom painting at St Peter's, Wenhaston

SOUTHWOLD, *Suffolk*
ST EDMUND

The church is dedicated to Edmund, a 9th-century king of East Anglia who was murdered by Viking raiders and became a popular native saint. Fire destroyed the original church on this site in 1430, and during the following decades a new building was raised in sumptuous Late Gothic style. Flushwork, that speciality of East Anglia (see Eye, page 76), is to be seen on all the exterior walls and buttresses, sometimes chequer-boarded, sometimes in panels. Above the west window of the tower, a shorthand Latin inscription in crowned flushwork letters spells out *SCT EDMUND ORA P NOBIS*, 'Pray for us St Edmund'.

Inside, the large Late Gothic windows suffuse the interior with light, thanks to the unexpected, but merciful, removal of their heavy Victorian stained glass by a German bomb in World War II. Only the east window was spared. Nave and chancel are continuous, interrupted only by the chancel screen which runs the full width of nave and aisles. Like most of the woodwork here, it is of a date with the church. The panels are well painted with 36 figures. Sadly, they bear the scars of post-Reformation fanaticism, being literally defaced. Special attention should be paid to the diaper patterns behind the figures. They are particularly delicate and inventive, painted in relief on gesso, a kind of plaster. St James, for example, has a background pattern of miniature shells, his emblem. Other contemporary woodwork includes the stalls and an excellent hammer-beam roof.

Two curiosities are worth noting: the round communion table, dating from the reign of Elizabeth, and a 15th-century bell jack.

NEARBY

Blythburgh, *Holy Trinity:* once the hub of a busy medieval town but now left stranded with a few cottages. One of the best 'wool' churches. Famous bench ends include personifications of the Seven Deadly Sins, and the Arms of the Holy Trinity.

Roof detail, Holy Trinity

Bramfield, *St Andrew:* detached round Norman tower, the rest mainly High Gothic. Thatched roof. Screen with some surviving figures.

Wenhaston, *St Peter:* work from several periods. Large Doom painted on wooden boards, *circa* 1520, originally fitted under the chancel arch. Though rustic, its style is direct and lively. Gaps in the painting show where the carved figures of the Rood group stood.

WEOBLEY, *Hereford and Worcester*
ST PETER AND ST PAUL

A typical amalgamation of work from several periods. Its most outstanding feature, literally and architecturally, is the stately 14th-century steeple which rises proudly above the timber-framed cottages of Weobley. For no apparent reason, it was built north-west of the nave rather than in the conventional position due west. It provides a textbook example of the High Gothic style. The first stage has three-light windows with reticulated tracery. Only the central light is pierced through. The others are blind, intended as frames for sculpture. The figures are now lost, but the carved brackets on which they stood are still to be seen.

The tower represents the last stage of building here. The earliest surviving work is an unremarkable Norman south doorway. From the second part of the 13th century there are the chancel arch and chancel, a triple lancet window, the south transept and piscina. The piers supporting the chancel arch are triple

statue, and may mark the position of a former altar. It undoubtedly belongs to a period of rebuilding in the first part of the 14th century which also produced the arcades with their octagonal piers and the north transept.

NEARBY

Brinsop, *St George:* building of first half of 13th century. Norman doorway, *circa* 1150, tympanum carved with St George and the Dragon in a style recalling Kilpeck (page 81), arch above of beasts and human figures. Fragments of 14th-century stained glass including one panel with the church's patron saint. Some wall paintings. Good stained glass from the 1920s, by Sir Ninian Comper.

Eardisley, *St Mary Magdalene:* font is an inadequate word for a dramatic piece of Norman sculpture, *circa* 1150, illustrating the Harrowing of Hell on one side and two men fighting with spear and sword on the other. It is one of the country's finest examples of Romanesque art.

A spear fight on the font at St Mary Magdalene

shafts, each with a fillet, a narrow flat band of stone running from top to bottom. South of the arch is a very richly decorated niche set under a crocketted gable. It has a bracket for a

Monnington on Wye, *St Mary the Virgin:* inside and out, a period piece from the second half of the 17th century. Carved Royal Arms of Charles II. Tower survives from 15th-century church.

WEST WALTON, *Norfolk*
ST MARY

For generations, this is the church that has been held up to students of art history as the epitome of Early Gothic architecture, and rightly so. Just about everything that meets the eye is from the years around 1240. But before you rush in to see the celebrated interior, spend a few minutes on the fine detached tower. Standing away from the church, the tower has arched entrances on all four sides, the north and south arches with generous dogtooth moulding, a favourite of the Early Gothic masons. The corner buttresses are polygonal in section, another distinguishing feature of the period. Each buttress has two large gabled niches on its lowest stage, and on the upper stages, tall, elegant blind arcading which continues right round the tower. The belfry has large two-light windows with plate tracery of a foiled circle.

The west door is an unusual find in a parish church. It has twin pointed arches set beneath a semicircular one, so that the doorway has a central shaft. The south porch is impressive, despite an incongruous brick gable, added in Tudor times. The large arched entrance, which is rich in dogtooth, is flanked by imperious polygonal buttresses with two stages of arcading in high relief. The capitals of the inner doorway have exceptionally lively stiff-leaf carving, another hallmark of Early Gothic style.

And so to the famous interior. It could not be called sumptuous: what it has is a haughty elegance in which each architectural element is coolly and precisely integrated into the overall composition. The only jarring note is the Late Gothic west window, which replaces a group of lancets. In the clerestory there is painted wall decoration simulating wall hangings with flowered patterns. The clerestory is arcaded in imitation of the nave arcades below. These have stiff-leaf carving in such high relief that the leaves appear about to curl off their capitals. Round piers with detached shafts and annulet rings complete the church's roll call of typical Early Gothic features.

Textbook Early Gothic architecture within St Mary's

NEARBY

Leverington, *St Leonard:* 13th- to 15th-century work. Impressive tower. Stained-glass Tree of Jesse with 61 figures, 13 of them complete 15th-century survivals.

Walsoken, *All Saints:* stately late Norman shading into Early Gothic. Good roof and other woodwork. Wooden statues of King David with harp and Solomon. Seven Sacraments font.

THE NORTH COUNTRY

St Andrew's, Roker

The crypt within St Mary's, Lastingham

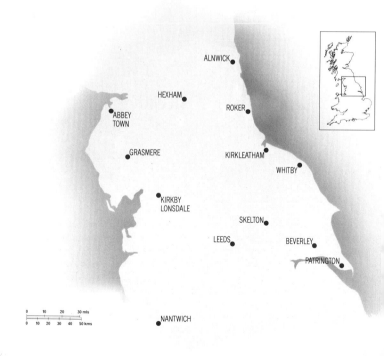

ALNWICK

HEXHAM

ROKER

ABBEY TOWN

GRASMERE

KIRKLEATHAM

WHITBY

KIRKBY LONSDALE

SKELTON

LEEDS

BEVERLEY

PATRINGTON

NANTWICH

| 0 | 10 | 20 | 30 mls |
| 0 | 10 | 20 | 30 | 40 | 50 kms |

ABBEY TOWN, *Cumbria*
ST MARY

This was formerly the church of Holme Cultram Abbey which was founded by the Cistercians in 1150. Only a fragment of the church remains: six bays of a nave which once stretched to nine. The piers are of eight attached shafts. Their capitals are modest, some having a flat broad-leafed design often called 'water-leaf', others completely plain. The use of pointed arches and water-leaf argues strongly for a date late in the 12th century. When aisles were added to a church, the first stage was to break through the old nave walls to make openings for the new arcade, but here there was a bizarre reversal of the normal sequence of events: the archways of the Norman arcades were walled up and set with windows on two levels.

The showpiece of this rather maimed church is the west porch. It was built by Robert Chamber, abbot here in the early 16th century. The use of dogtooth moulding is a deliberate anachronism, but one the Victorian revivalists would have applauded. Inside there are good fragments of sculpture and tracery of various dates, rescued, no doubt, from the ruined parts of the church. Pieces of the abbot's tomb bear his rebus (a personal emblem that was often a visual pun on the owner's name — in Chamber's case, a chained bear).

The west doorway is the best survival from the original church. Four orders of shafts, all with water-leaf capitals, support a richly moulded arch. On the inside of the west front there is a gallery set within the thickness of the wall. Similar west galleries are found in other monastic churches of this date (Dunstable Priory, for example — see page 42). They may have served a specific liturgical function, associated perhaps with antiphonal singing in which the choir was divided into sections which sang in different parts of the church.

NEARBY

Isel, *St Michael:* by the banks of the River Derwent. Norman, *circa* 1130. Mass dials. Fragments of pre-Conquest carvings, with Viking-inspired designs, including a 'triskele', a three-armed symbol of the Trinity.

Top: *The interior, St Michael's, Isel*
Above: *The church's Triskele Stone of circa 900*

Torpenhow, *St Michael:* 12th- and 13th-century work. Enthusiastic rather than sophisticated carved decoration produces an impression of rugged charm, compared with which the nave ceiling, dating to *circa* 1680 and painted with cupids and garlands of flowers, seems rather effete.

ALNWICK, *Northumberland*
ST MICHAEL AND ALL ANGELS
While the merchants of East Anglia and the West Country enjoyed the fruits of the wool trade and raised lavish Late Gothic churches in their peaceful towns, the inhabitants of this region fought a sporadic war with the Scots for some three centuries. Small wonder that there are few Late Gothic churches here of any note. Alnwick's church is the exception. Set on a hillside above the River Alne, it is a perfect example of a completely Late Gothic building.

In 1309, Alnwick Castle was acquired by the powerful Percy family, and it may be that their protection provided the local stability needed for church-building. In fact, the earliest feature of the church dates from this time: a pointed lancet with a trefoiled head in the west wall of the north aisle. Shortly afterwards, perhaps beginning before 1350, a programme of rebuilding produced the present north aisle and its windows, and the south arcade, which has octagonal piers and carved heads in the spandrels between the arches, one of them a splendid roaring lion.

In 1464, a second period of activity was initiated when Henry VI empowered the town to raise money from a toll to rebuild the church. To acknowledge their gratitude, the parish set up a wooden statue of Henry, rediscovered during one of three Victorian restorations. A second statue, possibly of St Sebastian or St Edmund, was found at the same time. Both are of rustic craftsmanship and have new heads. One window has a charming 15th-century roundel of the Pelican in her Piety, a popular medieval subject: a pelican pecks her breast to feed her young with her blood, an allegory of Christ's sacrifice on the Cross. The rest of the stained glass is a veritable trade directory of Victorian manufacturers. In all, seven different firms, including Clayton and Bell, give a good account of themselves.

NEARBY
Bamburgh, *St Aidan:* said to be built on the site of the Saxon church where Aidan died. Thirteenth century with alterations of 14th and 15th. Crypt. Hagioscope with stone tracery. In churchyard, Victorian Gothic shrine to Grace Darling, popular heroine of a shipwreck in 1838.

Warkworth, *St Lawrence:* 12th century with fine vaulted chancel. Tower *circa* 1200 with 14th-century broach spire. South aisle and porch 15th century or a little earlier. Saxon cross with interlace.

Recumbent effigy of a knight on the south wall of the nave at St Lawrence's

Effigy of knight *circa* 1330, cross legged and of unusually detailed craftsmanship. Seventeenth-century altar rails in wrought-iron.

BEVERLEY, *Humberside*
ST MARY

There is an embarrassment of riches in Beverley: not only the minster, which ranks among the finest Gothic churches of Europe, but also the Parish Church of St Mary, which can fairly claim to be one of England's best.

In the 13th century the Norman building was enlarged by extending the chancel and rebuilding the nave with aisles. Of this date is the crowning glory of the church: the chapel of St Michael in the north chancel aisle. It was built in

In addition to the fine collection within St Mary's, there are also misericords to be seen at Beverley Minster

1280 and has windows with late geometric tracery. The elaborately vaulted ceiling was added later by 'W Hal, Carpenter', whose signature appears on a boss carved with the masons' emblems of compasses, set square and axe. The roof of the chancel is dated 1445 and has panels painted with 40 Kings of England, some more legend than fact, ending with Henry VI, monarch of the day.

In 1520 tragedy struck. The Norman tower had been heightened, increasing the load on its supporting arches which had already been weakened by the 13th-century rebuilding of the nave. During a Sunday service the tower fell through the nave roof, killing several of the congregation. The church was very much used by the town's guilds, and it was from these guilds that

the money was raised to build a new tower and nave arcades. Their sponsorship is recorded by inscriptions on the hood moulds of the arcades. The hood mould stops may even be portraits of the donors. The eastern pier of the north arcade was paid for by the Guild of Minstrels, who had a yearly meeting here to choose their officials, and on it appear five of their company playing musical instruments. The church possesses an exceptionally fine collection of misericords dating from about 1450, 23 in all.

Outside, the tower, the south porch and the west front claim attention. The western façade was partly rebuilt in the 19th century by A W N Pugin, the pioneer of the Gothic Revival. The weather vane on top of the south-west turret is said to be his last design, sketched, so the story goes, on the back of an envelope.

NEARBY

Holme upon Spalding Moor, *All Saints:* set on a hill, a landmark for miles around. Splendid Late Gothic tower has niche with God the Father holding his saints in a napkin, a representation of the church's dedication. Seventeenth-century barrel organ.

Howden, *St Peter:* collegiate church of late 13th and early 14th centuries. Roofless chapter house. Ruined chancel. Harmonious Late Gothic interior with 15th-century reredos and a number of good monuments.

GRASMERE, *Cumbria*
ST OSWALD

This is Wordsworth country. The poet is buried in a corner of the churchyard, and his own description of St Oswald's serves as a fitting introduction:

Not raised in nice proportions was the pile,
But large and massy for duration built;
With pillars crowded and the roof upheld
by naked rafters intricately crossed.

Pebble dash envelops the exterior like a thick old overcoat, protecting it from the weather and giving away little of its history. The nave and tower would appear to be 14th century. The interior comes as a surprise: it is divided along its length by a most eccentric arcade to form twin naves. Outside there is no hint of this unusual arrangement as the nave has a single gabled roof. Moreover, the arcade has two tiers of arches, the lower tier dating from the middle of the 16th century, and the upper 100 years or so later. The arches are no more than primitive openings in a thick wall of masonry. Its rough-hewn surface is whitewashed and contrasts starkly with the blackened timbers of the roof which are indeed 'intricately crossed'. There are

two separate roof structures beneath one roof. Each has its own set of trusses resting on the bottoms of the upper arches of the central arcade.

The church still has its poor box, dated 1648, and there is a fragment of a Norman cross shaft carved with foliage, a standing figure and a stylised animal. Wordsworth's wall memorial is a profile medallion, carved by Thomas Woolner, with an epitaph by John Keble. Since the poet's day, nothing has changed. The church remains rough-cast and pragmatic yet, in its simple honesty, most moving.

NEARBY

Gosforth, *St Mary:* simple Norman church with nave, chancel and bellcote, much rebuilt during the 1890s in High Gothic style. Important examples of Saxon sculpture: cross in churchyard, 5m tall, has Viking influence in design and subject matter, pagan mythology one side, Christian the other; also two hog-back tombstones with battle scenes and the Crucifixion.

Millom, *Holy Trinity:* red sandstone church safely tucked away by the ruined walls of the castle. Late Norman with Gothic additions. Huddleston Chapel has interesting monuments.

St Oswald's, robust and rustic

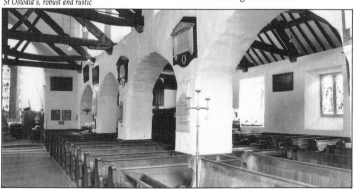

HEXHAM, *Northumberland*
ST ANDREW

Here is a church so long in history and so rich in interest that it is only possible to touch upon some of its more unusual features. The first church was built here *circa* 675 by Wilfrid, who had been sent out from Lindisfarne. According to contemporary writers it was miraculous in size, with many domes and porticos, and adorned with pictures and colours of wonderful variety. Of this magnificent building, only the crypt remains, but what a marvellously evocative place! Holiness seems built into the walls with the broken patterns and interrupted inscriptions of reused Roman stones.

Roman stones were used in the construction of ancient St Andrew's

Upstairs in the chancel is a Saxon stone chair, believed to be Wilfrid's throne. It is tub shaped and carved on each arm with an interlace pattern and a triangular knot — an abstract symbol of the indivisible Trinity. The chancel, built around 1200, is the most sumptuous part of the church and has elegant Early Gothic features. The nave was sacked by the Scots in 1296 and lay in ruins until it was rebuilt in 1907, when much work was done to put right an extensive but disastrous restoration of last century. Built into the new nave are many pieces of Roman and Saxon stonework.

A unique survival of monastic days is the night stair: 35 foot-worn steps down which the monks filed from the dormitory into the cold dark church for Matins. Below the landing at the top of the stairs is the slype, a passageway that led from the north-east corner of the cloister to the monks' cemetery. Set in the slype are two Roman altars and a massive monument to Flavinus, standard bearer to a Roman cavalry regiment. He is shown on horseback, riding down an enemy of Rome. The inscription reveals that he died at the age of only 25 after seven years' service, and commends his spirit 'to the gods of the shades'.

NEARBY

Blanchland, *St Mary:* formerly part of an abbey, it fell into ruin after the Dissolution, but the chancel, north transept and tower were rebuilt from 1752. Medieval coffin slabs with foliated crosses: an abbot's with chalice and pastoral staff, and a forester's with swords, bows and arrows. Churchyard cross with original traceried head.

Ovingham, *St Mary:* pre-Conquest tower. Good 13th-century work with chancel and transepts rich in lancets. Chancel north window has pretty roundels of birds, beasts, fishes and insects, 'all ye works of the Lord'. Fragments of Saxon cross. Medieval coffin slabs with emblems of trades.

KIRKBY LONSDALE, *Cumbria*
ST MARY

St Mary's is set in a churchyard with invigorating views of the fells captured by the painter Turner. Much of the tower was rebuilt at the start of the 18th century. The west side has a clock face set chirpily cock-eyed, partly obscuring an earlier window. At the bottom of the tower is the first clue to the church's history: an ornate, late Norman Romanesque doorway with two orders of shafts, chevron moulding and an arch with a cross-shaped pattern and figurative carving. The south doorway is of the same period.

St Mary's round piers are decorated with pronounced diamond patterns

Inside, it is again Norman work that catches the eye. The north arcade has three bays surviving from the early 12th century. The piers are alternately round and compound. The round piers are boldly incised with a diamond trellis pattern, copied directly from Durham Cathedral. The masons obviously set out with grand intentions. But something must have happened to prevent their ambitions being fulfilled. One of the capitals remains unfinished and, when work resumed later in the 12th century, the south arcade was more conventionally designed and built so close to the north arcade that the nave is uncomfortably narrow in proportion to the scale of the earlier piers. In fact, the aisles are wider than the nave, and, to increase further the width of the church, an outer aisle was added to the north in the Late Gothic period.

There is also Early Gothic work: three gently stepped lancets at the east end. The High Gothic style is represented by the reticulated tracery of the east windows of the south and inner north aisles. The result is a church of complex architectural history and great individuality.

NEARBY

Cartmel, *St Mary:* priory founded 1188, built during the late 12th, early 13th centuries. Upper stage of central tower set diagonally, a simple but effective piece of design. Late Gothic east window of stunning size. Good woodwork with fine collection of misericords. Fourteenth-century Harrington family monuments with very expressive weepers.

Crosthwaite, *St Kentigern:* mainly 16th-century Gothic with 14th-century chapel. Consecration crosses. Good monuments. Eighteenth-century pitch-pipe and baton used to keep metrical psalms in tune and time before the advent of church organs. Old rhyme warning bell-ringers that bad behaviour will incur a fine: 'and he that rings in either spur or hat, must pay his sixpence certainly for that . . . '

Witherslack, *St Paul:* 17th century, but heightened in the 18th. Routinely Gothic outside, calmly Classical in. Charming memorial with sleeping child.

KIRKLEATHAM, *Cleveland*
ST CUTHBERT

This dignified Classical church was mostly built in 1763. Set in a round-headed recess at the east end is a Venetian window, one of the most elegant motifs of the Classical Revival's repertoire. This is a three-light window in which the side openings are square topped and narrower than the central opening which has a semicircular head rising up above the level of the other lights. Inside, the roof is supported by two arcades or, more properly, colonnades of Tuscan columns. Much of the original furnishing survives and there are good grave slabs with handsome calligraphy.

Grafted on to the north side of the chancel is a Baroque mausoleum of such an extrovert design that it shouts down the quiet refinement of the church. It was built for the Turner family by James Gibbs in 1740. Like many young men of his day, Marwood William Turner set off for the Grand Tour of Italy, but he fell ill and died at Lyons. His father raised the mausoleum the following year. His memorial, by Peter Scheemakers, shows a studious youth leaning on a Classical pillar piled with books. The mausoleum is octagonal in plan with a circular window in each side. Rustication of the vermiculated variety, literally meaning 'worm-eaten', runs in wide bands around the building, giving it a fitting visual gravity. The roof is an octagonal pyramid with an urn for a finial and undercut at the base in order to emphasise its mass.

Marwood was not the only one here to die young. In the church is a moving little brass to Dorothy Turner who died at the age of four and is shown proudly wearing her grown-up

Classicism of the 18th century at St Cuthbert's, Kirkleatham

Elizabethan frock. More fortunate was Robert Coulthirst, whose fine brass commemorates a life of 90 years. Leaving the church, the skull and crossbones on the piers of the churchyard gate remind the visitor yet again that 'the life of Man is but a span'.

NEARBY

Billingham, *St Cuthbert:* pre-Conquest tower marooned in an industrial setting. Circular and star-shaped openings are unusual. Nave of Saxon proportions but with 12th-century rebuilding.

Easby, *St Agatha:* standing beside the ruined abbey, an aisless Norman church, 'modernised' in 13th century. Cast of 8th-century Easby Cross (the original is in the Victoria and Albert Museum). Chancel has excellent mid-13th-century wall paintings: in a typical example of medieval subject pairing (see Fairford, page 32), the story of the Fall from Grace in the Garden of Eden faces the story of the Redemption of Mankind through the birth and death of Christ. In the splays of the windows are Labours of the Months.

LEEDS, *West Yorkshire*
ST JOHN

St John's, in New Briggate, is the best of the many churches in Leeds. It was built between 1632 and 1634 at the expense of John Harrison, a rich cloth merchant. The stained glass of the east window shows him standing in the market earning the fortune that made the church possible. The founder lived to worship here for over 20 years. His monument is a modest wall plaque designed in simple Classical taste.

The chancel screen, St John's

The church is uncommonly large for its time: the reign of Charles I was no more a period of great confidence in church-building than it was in affairs of State. Its architecture is still resolutely Late Gothic. Inside, St John's is wide and spacious, lit by straight-topped windows divided into narrow lights with trefoiled heads. The south aisle is wide enough to be called a second nave. The roofs are supported on wooden corbels, carved and painted as angels, some with musical instruments.

Only the furnishings admit that times have changed since the late Middle Ages. The chancel screen, stretching across both naves, has balusters that taper elegantly towards the foot. Over both entrances are huge crests of open strapwork, which resemble pieces of a giant lace cravat, with cut-out obelisks standing on their scrolls.

Many of the churches in Leeds date from the 19th century. Among the better examples are: St Aidan, Roundhay Road, built in the Italian Romanesque style, with stunning mosaics of 1916 in the tradition of the Arts and Crafts Movement; St Bartholomew, Armley, Early Gothic style; St Saviour, Ellerby Road, High Gothic; and to complete the

catalogue of revivalist styles, the Late Gothic St Peter, Kirkgate. In 1938, the Church of the Epiphany in Gipton, by N F Cachemaille-Day, finally managed to loosen the shackles of revivalism.

NEARBY

Adel, *St John the Baptist:* jewel of a Norman village church now swamped by Leeds's suburban sprawl. Rich south door under gable with sculpture of

The sanctuary ring from the door of St John the Baptist

Christ in Majesty. Heraldic glass in vestry, 1681. Norman bronze door ring, finely crafted to represent a bear swallowing a man.

Birkin, *St Mary:* another complete Norman church but on a grander scale, with tower and vaulted apse.

NANTWICH, *Cheshire*
ST MARY

The church was built of the local red sandstone between about 1340 and the end of the century, bridging the transition between High and Late Gothic periods. It is the earlier style, however, that sets the luxurious tone. The central tower is octagonal, battlemented and set with a pinnacle at each of its corners. The bell-stage openings have plate tracery and, above, ogee hood moulds, heavy with crockets. Since the openings almost fill each face of the octagon, the hood moulds appear to garland the tower in a continuous sequence of sinuous ogee waves.

The chancel is the architectural highlight, both inside and out. North and south windows have beautiful High Gothic tracery. Above each window is a prominent hood mould, ogee shaped and crocketted, the point of the hood mould enclosing a quatrefoil set with a head — a portrait no doubt. Even though the east window is thoroughly Late Gothic in its tracery, the same hood mould shape is repeated on a larger scale so that the meeting point of the ogee curves pierces the parapet and rises above the battlements, creating a very dramatic effect.

Inside, piscina and sedilia are treated with the same richness of decoration. The magnificent set of choir stalls, dating from around 1390, have canopies sprinkled with gold stars, and inhabited by a choir and orchestra of angels. A good number have misericords. A wife threatening her husband with a ladle (reminiscent of a graffito at All Saints', Leighton Buzzard, page 59) appears among other familiar subjects: a virgin and unicorn, St George and the Dragon, a mermaid and fishes.

The superbly carved choir stalls at St Mary's, Nantwich

Less familiar are a devil forcing open a nun's mouth, and the skinning of a stag. Several scenes from the popular story of Reynard the Fox are also illustrated.

The chancel is roofed by an excellent timber lierne vault with carved bosses showing the Life of the Virgin, and the Nativity, Crucifixion and Resurrection of Christ. From the central boss at the east end, God the Father presides over all.

NEARBY

Acton, *St Mary:* brown stone church of mainly 13th and 15th centuries with much 18th-century rebuilding, including tower in Gothic style. Fragments of stonework with primitive Norman carving.

Malpas, *St Oswald:* 18th-century iron gates lead to a church of mixed High and Late Gothic work. Superb nave roof with plenty of bosses and flying angels. Good alabaster effigies, 1522, of Randolph Brereton and wife, their pet dog nibbling at the hem of her dress. Bronze tablet to Charles Woolley Dod, 1904, Art Nouveau style.

PATRINGTON, *Humberside*
ST PATRICK

The regal bearing of this church has earned it the justifiable nickname, 'Queen of Holderness'. It is indeed one of the country's very finest High Gothic churches, begun towards the end of the 13th century and completed in the early 14th. The slender spire, which gives it such an air of nobility, was added 100 years later. The transition from square tower to octagonal spire is achieved most elegantly by a screen of open traceried panels encircling the base of the spire like a tall crown.

Inside, the grandeur and unity of the design are still more evident. There are east and west aisles in both transepts, a refinement normally found only in cathedrals. Yet, surprisingly, there is no clerestory. Piers with clustered shafts meet the eye like a forest in all directions. Some of them have masons' marks. Their capitals are

St Patrick's, crowned by its elegant, soaring spire

Church building on a large scale at Holy Trinity

carved with densely packed foliage, no longer the stylised forms of Early Gothic, but leaves that are naturalistic enough to be recognisable species. The chancel has excellent sedilia and piscina, rich in crockets, ogee arches and pinnacles. Opposite is an Easter sepulchre of rare elaboration. Its lower part is carved with sleeping soldiers in contemporary armour; the central part shows Christ stepping from His coffin with angels on either side swinging censers (containers for burning incense); the upper part, likely to have been an Ascension scene, is now lost.

The church's windows present a fine illustration of the development of High Gothic tracery. The transepts were built first and have 'geometric' tracery featuring convex triangles; next, the aisles with 'flowing' tracery; and then the west window which has 'flamboyant' tracery, or at least the nearest English masons ever came to the flamboyant tracery of Continental churches before it was superseded by Late Gothic tracery, like that of the great east window.

NEARBY

Hedon, *St Augustine:* known as the 'King of Holderness'. Mostly Early Gothic with later tower of great splendour. Stiff-leaf capitals in nave. Nineteenth-century rose window by G E Street.

Kingston upon Hull (Hull), *Holy Trinity:* huge church with 14th-century chancel and transepts built of brick, exceptionally early use of this material. Large Late Gothic windows almost eliminate solid walling. Tower, *circa* 1500, with fine oak star vault. Many monuments, including that of William de la Pole, 1366, said to be the richest merchant in England.

ROKER, *Tyne and Wear*
ST ANDREW

Built between 1906 and 1907, this is the first church of the century to tread the tightrope between tradition and modernism. The result is not a sterile compromise but a triumph of originality. The architect was Edward Prior, 20 years earlier one of the founders of the Arts and Crafts Movement.

As a whole the building has a Gothic resonance, but its parts and their arrangement are not 'correct' Gothic in the sense of Victorian Revivalism. The tower, for example, has diamond-shaped buttresses and is placed, not centrally, nor at the west end of the nave, but over the western part of the chancel. Window tracery is retained as an idea, but rationalised into straight criss-cross patterns, paradoxically recalling the pilaster strip decoration of pre-Conquest building.

Inside, the nave is divided into bays by majestic parabolic arches rising from dwarf piers and meeting in a point at the roof ridge to create a cavernous space like the belly of Jonah's whale. The design seems to have been inspired by medieval timber construction, but its materials are modern: the arches are of reinforced concrete faced with a local limestone, and even some of the major 'timbers' of the roof are, in fact, cast

St Andrew's architecture, a fine balance of old and new influences

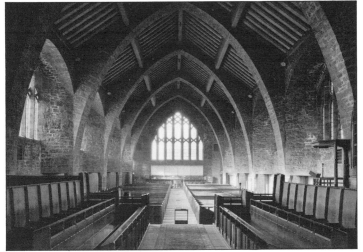

The spacious, uncluttered interior, St Andrew's

concrete — a sleight of hand that must have raised a few eyebrows among the purists of the Arts and Crafts Movement. One of the Movement's leading craftsmen, Ernest Grimson, created the beautiful polished wrought-iron altar furnishings and a stylish lectern, inlaid on its triangular sides with a graceful floral pattern in mother-of-pearl, ivory, ebony and silver. The chancel carpet and the tapestry reredos, showing the Adoration of the Magi, were produced by William Morris's workshop, the reredos to designs by Edward Burne-Jones. The sumptuous stained glass of the east window is by Humphrey Payne.

NEARBY

Monkwearmouth, *St Peter and St Cuthbert:* built 7th century, sacked by Vikings. Rebuilt and then sacked by Normans. Now beset by decaying industrialism. Tower and west wall of pre-Conquest church survive. Fragments of Saxon carving.

Saxon architecture survives at St Peter and St Cuthbert

Seaham, *St Mary:* early 8th-century nave with herringbone masonry and reused Roman stones. Chancel, tower and porch of 13th century. Eighteenth-century sundial contains an inscription, a wry ode to 'the natural clock-work by the Mighty One'.

SKELTON, *North Yorkshire*
ST GILES

Set in a village on the northern fringe of York, St Giles's gives a near-perfect glimpse of the small Early Gothic parish church. It was built around 1240. With no later structural additions and only the most sympathetic of restorations (between 1814 and 1818 by Henry Graham at the tender age of 19), the church stands today much as its master mason intended. The unity and refinement of the work suggest the influence of the York masons only four miles away. The stiff-leaf capitals of the deeply recessed south doorway have a particular maturity, although it is now difficult to judge how much they owe to the hand of Henry Graham.

The church's ground plan is devised with an economy that sets the tone for the elegant simplicity of the whole building. A basic rectangle is divided by arcades running the length of the building. They mark off narrow aisles which share the same steeply pitched roof as the nave. The arcade piers are of four attached shafts with fillets and bell capitals enriched with a band of nailhead moulding. The chancel arch is only distinguished from the arcade arches by a hood mould with nailhead decoration. There is nailhead too on the string course that runs around the inside walls, looping over the pointed windows to form hood moulds, and ending in foliage bosses.

In the chancel is a pretty piscina with tiny leaf decoration and a fluted bowl. The grouped lancet windows have dogtooth moulding in two sizes and are framed by detached shafts with annulet rings. Few Gothic churches of such small dimensions boast the purity of style found at St Giles's.

NEARBY

Nun Monckton, *St Mary:* nave of a former 12th- and 13th-century nunnery. West door with five orders in Transitional style. Remains of sculpture in niches. Stunning display of lancets. A textbook example of the Victorians' favourite period: middle Early Gothic.

York: besides the minster, there are 19 medieval parish churches here, some of them now redundant. Their architecture is mostly of the prosperous 15th and 16th centuries. All Saints' in North Street has a remarkable group of windows which include the Nine Orders of Angels, the Seven Acts of Mercy, and the 'Pricke of Conscience' window which illustrates a poem about the calamitous events of the last 15 days heralding the World's end.

Detail from a window, the 'Last 15 days of the World', at All Saints

WHITBY
ST MARY, North Yorkshire

High on the cliffs overlooking the fishing port, the low nave and squat tower seem to crouch down out of the wind. One hundred and ninety-nine steps lead up from the town to this rugged church, which is mainly of the late 12th century, with an Early Gothic transept. Rectangular Georgian

Space utilisation at the extreme within St Mary's, designed to accommodate a large congregation

St Mary's overlooks Whitby harbour

windows, white painted and domestic, sit rather uncomfortably beside round-headed Norman doorways. Through their clear panes, glimpses of wooden staircases prepare the visitor for what is to be found inside.

During the 17th and 18th centuries the interior was progressively filled with a haphazard assortment of box pews and galleries, rising almost to the ceiling. This was how the auditory plan, upon which the new Classical churches were being built, was translated into the setting of a medieval building. The emphasis in worship had shifted from the Mass to the sermon. Here the galleries were crowded in at all angles so that everyone could see and hear the preacher in the pulpit. It is said that the church could seat a congregation of 2,000. The pulpit, of 1778, has a reader's desk and a tester with a crown of scroll-like leaves supporting a pineapple.

A flat boarded ceiling with a skylight bears down over the galleries, giving the claustrophobic impression of the lower deck of a sailing ship. Even the Rood screen is gone, its place usurped by the Cholmely family pew, set up on twisted 'barley-sugar' columns with its back turned to the gloomy chancel, a symbol of the de-mystified religion of the Age of Enlightenment. The interior is more a social document than a work of art, but it is enormously appealing for all that, and an evocative illustration of how most Gothic churches wintered through the 18th century before being 'corrected' to their medieval arrangement by Victorian restoration.

NEARBY

Lastingham, *St Mary:* outstanding crypt of 11th century with nine groined vaults on four sturdy piers and an apse at the east end, virtually a church in itself. Many fragments of Saxon sculpture.

Pickering, *St Peter and St Paul:* extensive 15th-century wall paintings provide an excellent impression of how medieval churches must have looked, though their artistic quality is coarsened by restoration; less familiar subjects like Herod's Feast are among old favourites like St Christopher.

SCOTLAND

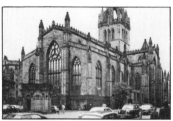

St Giles's, Edinburgh

The nave, Glasgow Cathedral

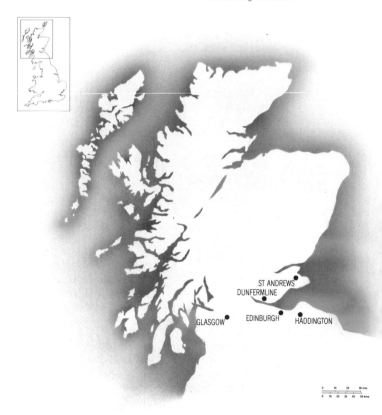

ST ANDREWS

DUNFERMLINE

GLASGOW

EDINBURGH

HADDINGTON

DUNFERMLINE, *Fife*
ABBEY OF THE HOLY TRINITY

A priory was founded here by Malcolm and Margaret Canmore. The foundations of a 13th-century shrine to Margaret can still be seen at the east end of the church. In 1128 David I promoted the priory to the status of an abbey, and a campaign of rebuilding was begun that lasted until the middle of the 12th century. The nave of the church belongs to this period. The west front was designed as the main façade with a rich west doorway and twin towers, but the years have not been kind. A High Gothic window was inserted above the door in the 14th century; in the 16th, unwieldy buttresses were built against it; a little later the north tower was rebuilt and a spire added; and in the 19th century the

Different styles of decoration on the piers within the Abbey of the Holy Trinity

south tower was demolished by lightning and had to be rebuilt. The eastern parts of the church fared even worse. Chancel and transepts were sacked by Reformers and left in ruins until the 19th century, when a new east end was built by William Burn.

The nave interior is in the finest tradition of the austere, monumental Romanesque style, the best example of its kind in Scotland. It has six-bay arcades of round piers with water-leaf capitals, clerestory and triforium — a mark of architectural ambition in the 12th century. The eastern piers have deeply incised zigzag patterns around their circumferences. The aisles are vaulted and their walls decorated with blind arcading.

By contrast, the 19th-century parts seem rather pretentious. The tower in particular, with its balustrade spelling out 'King Robert the Bruce' like an advertising hoarding, cannot be seen as a sensitive design. The legendary Bruce was buried in the chancel in 1329, and now lies beneath an elaborate modern brass beside the pulpit.

NEARBY

Dunblane, *Dunblane Cathedral:* notable Early Gothic building with a tall, primitive tower 200 years older. West front with needle-sharp lancets and blind arcading. Fragments of early carving. Good carved choir stalls of *circa* 1447. Memorial slabs to three sisters who were all poisoned.

Stirling, *Holy Rood:* early 14th-century nave with original roof. Chancel with polygonal apse from early 16th century. Mary Queen of Scots and James VI (James I of England) were crowned here as babies. Tower bears the scars of gunshot from siege of 1651 when General Monck captured the town.

EDINBURGH, *Lothian*
ST GILES

There has been a church on this site since the 9th century. Of the Norman church built around 1120, only the four massive octagonal pillars supporting the central tower remain. The rest of the building was destroyed when Richard II sacked Edinburgh in 1385. As it stands today the church is mostly a rebuilding of the 15th century.

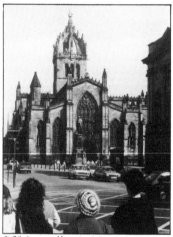

St Giles's, crowned by an ornate tower

St Giles's is the most impressive of the city's churches, thanks in large part to the late 15th-century tower, over 49m tall and topped by an open-work crown. The crown is formed by four flying buttresses curving inwards from the corners of the tower to meet in the middle where they support a single large pinnacle. Smaller pinnacles stand on the flying buttresses. This is an architectural feature that is unique to Scotland: two other examples survive.

In 1556, the church suffered badly at the hands of the Reformers: much of its decoration and many fittings,

including 44 altars, were destroyed. The church was split up to house four different congregations and remained so until its restoration in the late 19th century. John Knox was minister here until he died in 1572. The pulpit from which he preached is carved with scenes of the Acts of Mercy. There are monuments to many famous Scots, among them a bronze wall memorial to Robert Louis Stevenson.

Overlooking the city, Greyfriar's Churchyard is rich in Scottish religious history and should not be missed. It was here, on March 1st, 1638, that the National Covenant was signed, a formal undertaking to oppose the 'corruptions' of the Anglican faith which Charles I had imposed on Scotland. Forty years later the churchyard was used in the dead of winter as an open prison for 1,200 Covenanters, many of whom died. A memorial to the martyrs can be seen within the churchyard.

NEARBY

Abercorn, *St Serf:* 12th-century two-cell plan, remodelled in late 16th century and restored 1838. Celtic cross shaft. Hog's-back tomb. Blocked-up Norman doorway has carved tympanum, one of only two in Scotland. Medieval pulpit.

Dalmeny, *St Cuthbert:* best-preserved Scottish Norman church. South doorway arch carved with Agnus Dei and Signs of Zodiac, above blind arcading. Semicircular apse with stone vault. North aisle added in 1671.

Linlithgow, *St Michael:* large High Gothic church, finished 1242 but partly rebuilt after a fire in 1424. Tower and apse not completed until 1821. Open-work crown was lost from tower in the 19th century and replaced by one of modern design, the work of Geoffrey Clarke, in 1964.

GLASGOW, *Strathclyde*
ST MUNGO

Glasgow Cathedral is built on a site that slopes down to the east, so that the chancel and crypt beneath virtually form a two-storey edifice: the Upper Church and the Lower Church. The crypt or Lower Church is the richest part of the building and serves as the parish church.

The nave, Glasgow Cathedral

There is a long history to the building. A church was founded here by St Mungo in the 6th century. Between 1123 and 1132 that church was replaced by a cathedral, but this building burned down at the end of that century and was rebuilt. Of this rebuilding just one pier of the crypt remains. From 1233 to 1258, Bishop de Bondington replaced the

crypt, chancel and tower, all splendid Early Gothic work. More work was done during the 15th century, the nave being completed as late as 1480.

The Lower Church is considered to be one of the very best vaulted crypts of Gothic Europe. It has a grace and sense of proportion not normally associated with crypts. In the centre is the simple tomb of St Mungo, who was buried on this site by an ancient well in 603. There are four chapels, in one, an effigy of Bishop Wischard who crowned Robert the Bruce. To the north-east is the old Chapter House, described in Scott's *Rob Roy* — one of its pillars is now named after the hero. Here also is a bell of 1594 and a memorial slab to nine martyred Covenanters.

Among Glasgow's other churches, St Andrew's, of the mid-18th century, has an impressive Classical west front with a central steeple and an equally elegant interior. Representing the 19th century are St George's Tron Church by William Stark, 1807, and St David's, built in 1824 by Thomas Rickman, one of the main pioneers of the Gothic Revival.

NEARBY

East Kilbride: the first of Scotland's new 'satellite' towns has two modern churches. St Mark's Episcopal Church, 1956, with triangular elevations, and the Church of Scotland, 1964, built on a seven-sided plan.

Paisley, *Abbey Church:* founded 1163, but destroyed by English army of Edward I in 1307. Present building is of mid-15th and late 19th centuries. West front has deeply recessed doorway with elegant windows above. St Mirren's Chapel, built in 1499, houses 12th-century panels carved with scenes of the saint's life, and an effigy said to be of Robert the Bruce's daughter, Marjory.

HADDINGTON, *Lothian*
ST MARY

St Mary's window tracery has more in common with French than English styles

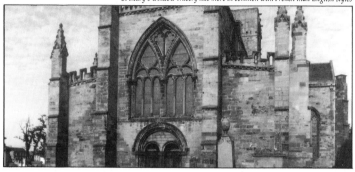

Like so many others north of the border, this 15th-century church spent many years in partial ruin, but the nave was always maintained as the parish church and in recent years the eastern parts of the church have been restored. The plan is cruciform with aisles in both nave and chancel. The arcades have piers with clustered shafts and capitals with copious foliage, naturalistically carved. At the west end is a fine double doorway under a round arch. The window tracery is of special interest. At this date in England, the flowing tracery of the High Gothic period had been replaced by the regimented panel-like tracery of Late Gothic. But this did not happen in Scotland. Here window tracery continued to develop along more flamboyant lines, as it did in Europe, especially France which had many important historical links with Scotland. The window tracery at St Mary's is a rare example of the Scottish flamboyant style.

The central tower is well decorated and shows some inventive design. For example, the transoms of the three tall bell openings are extended beyond the confines of the windows to form a string course encircling the tower walls. There are canopied niches for sculpture, now lost, of course, and good gargoyles. The tower was formerly topped by an open-work crown which housed a lantern and earned the church its nickname: the 'Lamp of Lothian'.

Also in Haddington is the almost perfect little Norman village church of St Martin, built on the two-cell plan. In the 13th century an upper chamber was added to the chancel.

NEARBY

Dunglass, *Collegiate Church:* a 15th-century church of rough-hewn looks with short central tower, but having much good detailed work. Sedilia with ornate decoration, including two angel corbels. Chancel walls curve over to produce a cave-like barrel vault. At one period the building was used as a stable by the local hunting fraternity.

Seton, *Collegiate Chapel:* built between 1478 and 1558. Cruciform with a blunt, possibly unfinished spire. Monument to Lord Seton who built the transepts and who fell at the Battle of Flodden, 1513. Barrel-vaulted chancel ending in three-sided apse. Some good window tracery. The nave was never built.

ST ANDREWS, *Fife*
HOLY TRINITY

In 1547, John Knox climbed up into the pulpit to preach his first public sermon in this beautiful and spacious building. The church was founded in 1412 but, like many others, has a chequered history. A rebuilding of 1799 was the last, and most drastic, of many alterations that left the original 15th-century form of the church almost unrecognisable. Between 1906 and 1909, MacGregor Chalmers, working from old drawings and from the archaeological evidence of the building itself, pieced together the restoration that is the church seen today. The stained glass, designed by Douglas Strachen, was added window by window during the 40 years following Chalmer's restoration.

Of the church's medieval fittings virtually nothing remains: just two choir stalls of around 1505 survived the destructive zeal of the Reformers. The Playfair aisle has some interesting memorials to Sir Nigel and other members of the family after whom it is named. A grand 18th-century marble monument to Archbishop Sharp shows a graphic scene of his murder in 1799, accompanied by a verbose inscription. There are curious reminders of a more repressive age: two repentance stools and a scold's bridle. And for the visitor who has strayed in off the golf course, there is the wall memorial to 'Old Tom' Harris, the famous golfer.

Also in St Andrews are the remains of the Norman Church of St Rule. A tall and primitive-looking tower, of around 1160, provides the visual focus of a romantic ruin. On its eastern wall the marks of three different roof lines can clearly be seen, evidence of the successive rebuildings of the chancel.

The three different roof lines at St Rule's are clearly visible in the tower's masonry

NEARBY

Crail, *St Mary:* 13th-century church of a pretty fishing village. Seventeenth-century woodwork. Painting of sailor using a sextant in chancel. Pre-Conquest cross. In churchyard, solid square building erected for securing the dead recalls the days of body-snatchers.

Leuchars, *St Athernase:* fine late 12th-century church with much rich carving. Chancel has apse with two tiers of blind arcading and 17th-century bellcote. Octagonal tower crowned by a lantern is of 17th century too.

Pittenweem *St Adrian:* probably a chapel of the lost priory. The 16th-century tower has a military bearing, and a chamber used as an old prison. Nearby is the cave shrine of St Fillan.

GLOSSARY

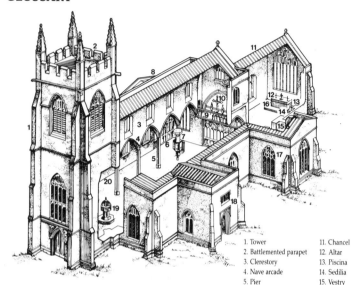

TYPICAL GOTHIC PARISH CHURCH

1. Tower
2. Battlemented parapet
3. Clerestory
4. Nave arcade
5. Pier
6. Parclose screen
7. Pulpit
8. Nave
9. Rood loft
10. Rood
11. Chancel
12. Altar
13. Piscina
14. Sedilia
15. Vestry
16. Sanctuary
17. Transept
18. Porch
19. Font
20. Aisle

Abacus. Flat slab of stone forming the top part of a capital.

Ambulatory. An aisle or processional walkway behind the high altar or around a cloister.

Annulet. Narrow ring of stone or metal encircling a column or shaft.

Apse. Semicircular or polygonal end to the chancel, or sometimes a transept.

Arcade. Series of arches supported on columns or pillars. Usually open, like the arcade that separates an aisle from the nave of a church, but sometimes used as relief decoration on a wall, in which case the term blind arcading is used.

Ashlar. Outer layer of comparatively thin squared stone blocks providing a smooth facing to rubble or brick walls.

Auditory plan. Church layout devised in the 17th century in which the pulpit is most prominent and the seating of the congregation arranged so that all could see and hear clearly.

Aumbry. Small recess in chancel wall, sometimes with a door, where the vessels used to celebrate Mass were kept.

Ball-flower. Decorative moulding typical of the High Gothic period made up of globular flowers formed by three petals enclosing a small ball.

Bay. Space between two piers or columns in an arcade.

Beakhead. Strikingly decorative moulding of the Norman period made up of the stylised heads of birds and animals.

Billet. Another Norman moulding, this one formed by a chequer-board of raised rectangles.

Blind arcading. See **arcade**.

Boss. Ornamental carving which disguises the meeting point of ribs in a stone vault or wooden roof.

Box pew. Seating enclosed by wooden panelling to protect the congregation from draughts.

Broach spire. Spire whose octagonal cross section is adapted to fit the square top of the tower by adding an elongated half-pyramid, called a broach, at each of the four corners.

Buttress. Vertical mass of masonry built at right angles to an outside wall to provide support or to counteract the outward thrust from an arch on the inside of the wall. See also **flying buttress.**

Cable moulding. Decoration typical of the Norman and Early Gothic periods which resembles intertwined string or thick rope.

Capital. Top part of a column or pillar. The carving of a capital, which may be very elaborate, gives a good clue to its architectural period.

Ceilure (or **cellure**). Area of roof above the altar or Rood screen which is more richly decorated than the rest.

Chancel. The eastern part of the church housing the altar, often separated from the nave by a chancel or Rood screen.

Chantry chapel. Small chapel within a church, founded by an individual or a guild who endowed the church with an income to pay for the saying of Masses for their souls after death. The chapel often contains the benefactor's tomb.

Chevron. A continuous zigzag pattern, most common decorative moulding of the Norman period.

Cinquefoil. See **foil.**

Clerestory. Row of windows pierced through the upper walls of the nave above the roofs of the aisles.

Consecration cross. One of a set of 12 crosses marked on the inside and outside walls of a church during the ceremony of consecration.

Corbel. A projecting block of stone set deeply into a wall. The projecting part is designed to support an arch or beam and is often carved as an angel or face.

Corbel table. A row of corbels supporting the eaves of a roof.

Cornice. The upper projecting part of an entablature in Classical architecture; a continuous horizontal projecting course or moulding at the top of a wall, building, etc.

Crockets. Decoration carved like buds or curled leaves and set regularly along the sloping sides of gables, canopies, spires and pinnacles, especially popular during the High Gothic period.

Crypt. Underground chamber beneath the chancel, usually vaulted.

Cusp. Projecting point between the foils of tracery in Gothic arches and windows.

Decalogue. The Ten Commandments.

Diaper. Regular pattern of square or diamond-shaped motifs painted or carved in low relief.

Dogtooth. A decorative moulding common during the Early Gothic period, made up of rows of four tooth-shaped motifs set together to form a diagonal cross.

Doom. Dramatic representation of the Last Judgement, usually painted over the chancel arch.

Dripstone. Raised stone moulding around a doorway or window, designed to throw off rainwater. Also known as a hood mould or label.

Easter sepulchre. Recess in chancel wall

(contd over page)

which held the consecrated host during Easter, symbolising the entombment of Christ. Usually richly ornamented.

Entablature. Classical architecture; the beam spanning two or more columns.

Fillet. A narrow flat band of stone running the length of a shaft.

Finial. Ornamental termination, usually foliated, found as a matter of course on pinnacles, bench-ends, etc.

Flushwork. Cut flints set into plain stonework to form a decorative pattern.

Flying buttress. Open half-arch which acts as a buttress by spanning across the roof of an aisle to carry the thrust of an upper wall down to a main buttress on the outer wall.

Foil. Space between cusps of tracery. Traceried arches and openings are often described by the number of their foils: a trefoil having three, a quatrefoil four, etc.

Foliated. Having a leaf-like form or decoration.

Four-leafed flower. Typical High Gothic moulding of square-ish flowers set in rows, each made of four leaves with a small ball at the centre.

Funerary hatchment or **escutcheon.** The arms of a deceased person painted on a diamond-shaped board and hung in the church after the funeral.

Gargoyle. A stone water-spout draining a gutter, usually carved as a hideous face or animal.

Hagioscope. See **squint.**

Hammer-beam. A particular type of roof construction in which the vertical and arch-braced timbers stand on horizontal beams projecting from the walls.

Hood mould. See **dripstone.**

Label. See **dripstone.**

Lancet. Tall and narrow pointed window typical of the Early Gothic period, often set in groups of three or five.

Laudian rails. Low railings of wood or iron set around the altar, introduced by Archbishop Laud in the 17th century.

Lesene. Narrow band of flat stone used to decorate walls in pre-Conquest architecture.

Lierne vault. See **vault.**

Light. Small window opening, or division within a larger window created by the vertical mullions.

'Long and short' work. Stone construction used to strengthen the corners of a building, common in Saxon building.

Lych gate. Roofed gateway to churchyard.

Mason's mark. Mark incised on a stone as a signature by the mason who worked it.

Mass dial. Sundial scratched on a south-facing wall with radiating lines to indicate the hours of church services.

Misericord. Bracket projecting from the underside of a hinged seat in the choir stalls, originally meant to give support to monks standing during long services and usually richly carved.

Mullions. Vertical stone bars dividing a window into lights and branching into tracery at the top of the window.

Nailhead. An Early Gothic decorative moulding consisting of a row of low pyramids rather like the heads of nails.

Nave. The main part of the church for use by the laity.

Niche. Shallow recess for a statue etc.

Ogee. Arch formed by two shallow S-shaped curves meeting in a point at the top, a feature introduced during the High Gothic period.

Order. Name for a particular design of Classical column and entablature. There were three Greek orders: Doric, Ionic and Corinthian. The Romans added two more: Tuscan and Composite.

Parclose. Wooden screen dividing an aisle or chapel from the main church.

Pediment. Low-pitched gable in Classical architecture.

Pier. Tall, freestanding pile of masonry supporting an arch or vaulting. The design of its cross section reflects its architectural period.

Pilaster. Shallow rectangular pier attached to a wall, usually a decorative rather than structural feature.

Pilaster strip. See **lesene.**

Pinnacle. A decorative pyramid or cone-shaped feature crowning towers, gables and buttresses, usually encrusted with crockets and topped by a finial.

Piscina. Small sink set in a recess in the chancel wall for the draining of water used by the priest to wash his hands during the Mass.

Poppyhead. Foliated or floral finial on a bench end or choir stall.

Portico. Low-pitched gable supported by a row of columns called a colonnade.

Quatrefoil. See **foil.**

Reredos. Ornamental screen, hanging or painting behind the altar.

Respond. Half-pillar attached to the wall at the end of an arcade to support the last arch.

Rood. Old English name for the Cross, in medieval times taken to mean the Crucifixion group including the Virgin Mary and St John.

Rood screen. Screen separating the chancel from the nave, and originally supporting the Rood loft with its representation of the Crucifixion. The screen was usually beautifully carved and painted.

Rose window. Circular window with radiating tracery.

Saddleback roof. Short gabled roof of a tower.

Sanctuary. The part of the chancel immediately surrounding the altar.

Sedilia. Seats for the clergy set in the south wall of the chancel. There are usually three of them and they are sometimes grouped with the piscina to form a single architectural unit.

Set-off. Sloping surface on buttresses, sills, etc to throw off rainwater.

Spandrel. Roughly triangular area of wall between adjacent arches of an arcade, or between the curve of an arched window, or doorway, and the square dripstone surrounding it.

Squint or **hagioscope.** Narrow opening in a wall or pillar giving a view into the chancel from a transept or aisle.

Stiff-leaf. Particularly stylised form of foliage decoration common on capitals of the Early Gothic period. The leaves stand upright and curl over at the top.

Strapwork. Decorative scroll-work of flat straps, painted or carved, much favoured in the Jacobean period.

String course. Plain or decorative moulding running horizontally along a church wall, often level with the springing point of the window arches. Also used to mark the stages of a tower.

Stucco. Ornamental plasterwork found in Classical and Baroque architecture.

Tester. Canopy or sounding board over a pulpit.

Tierceron vault. See **vault.**

Tracery. Ribs of stonework curving and intersecting to form a decorative network in the upper parts of windows and in screens and panelling. Window tracery provides a useful key to dating.

Transept. The parts to the north and south of the nave equivalent to the arms of the cross in a church built on the cruciform plan.

Transom. Horizontal bar across a window.

Trefoil. See **foil.**

Triforium. Arcaded gallery or section of blind arcading set above the nave arcade and below the clerestory, rarely found in parish churches.

Tympanum. Semicircular area defined by the straight lintel of a doorway and the curve of an arch above it, or a semicircle of wooden boards cut to fill in an archway. The former was usually richly carved; the latter painted with the scene of the Last Judgement.

Vault. Arched roof built of stone or brick. The barrel or tunnel vault with a semicircular cross section is the simplest type. Groined vaults are formed by the intersection of two barrel vaults at right angles, the groins being the lines of intersection. A quadri-partite vault is divided into four equal parts by two diagonal ribs. Sex-partite vaults are created by adding a third transverse rib to make six divisions. Further elaborations were achieved by adding ribs more for decorative than structural purposes. Tierceron ribs spring from the same point as the main ribs but instead of crossing the vault they meet obliquely. Lierne ribs, whose purpose is purely decorative, are short linking ribs. Most spectacular of all is the fan vault which has numerous ribs of equal length and curvature forming fan-like patterns over inverted cones of masonry.

Voussoirs. The wedge-shaped stones that fit together to make an arch.

Wagon roof. Roof built with curved rafters, reminiscent of the awning over the old-fashioned wagon.

Weepers. Small carved figures, usually angels, in niches round sides of tomb.

FURTHER READING

For detailed drawings, description and history of a particular church the best sources are the county-by-county volumes of *The Royal Commission on Historic Monuments* (HMSO) and *The Victoria County History* series (Oxford University Press) available in most public reference libraries.

The Buildings of England (Penguin, 1951 onwards), by Nikolaus Pevsner, also in volumes by county, give authoritative but rather dry descriptions of all churches of interest. *The Buildings of Scotland* (Penguin, 1984), edited by Colin McWilliam, and *The Buildings of Wales* (Penguin, 1986), by Edward Hubbard, follow the Pevsner tradition. *Collins Guide to the Parish Churches of England* (Collins, 1958), edited by John Betjeman provides a county-by-county guide in a single volume.

Books to read for the general history of parish churches include:

M D **Anderson,** *Looking for History in British Churches,* J Murray, 1951.

T D **Atkinson,** *English Architecture,* Methuen, 1963.

Francis **Bond,** *Screens and Galleries in English Parish Churches,* Oxford University Press, 1909.

T **Borenius and** E W **Tristram,** *English Medieval Painting,* Pegasus Press, 1927 (1977 facsimile edition by Hacker Art Books).

Hugh **Braun,** *Parish Churches: their Architectural Development,* Faber & Faber, 1970.

Frederick **Burgess,** *English Churchyard Memorials,* SPCK, 1979.

C J P **Cave,** *Roof Bosses in Medieval Churches,* Cambridge University Press, 1948.

Basil F **Clarke,** *Church Builders of the Nineteenth Century,* SPCK, 1938 (1969 facsimile edition by David & Charles).

Basil F **Clarke,** *Parish Churches of London,* Batsford, 1966.

Kenneth Clarke, *The Gothic Revival,* Constable, 1950.

Alec Clifton-Taylor, *English Parish Churches as Works of Art,* Batsford, 1974.

J Charles Cox, *Bench Ends in English Churches,* Oxford University Press, 1916.

F H Crossley, *English Church Monuments, 1150—1550,* Batsford, 1921.

John G Dunbar, *The Architecture of Scotland,* Batsford, 1966.

Katherine A Esdaile, *English Church Monuments, 1510—1840,* Batsford, 1946.

Richard Foster, *Discovering English Churches,* BBC Books/OUP New York, 1981.

Marshall Laird, *English Misericords,* John Murray, 1986.

S L Ollard & Gordon Cross, *A Dictionary of English Church History,* A R Mowbray, 1912.

Colin Platt, *The Parish Churches of Medieval England,* Secker & Warburg, 1981.

R W Soden, *Welsh Parish Churches,* Gomer Press, 1984.

E Tyrell-Green, *Parish Church Architecture,* SPCK, 1924.

T W West, *A History of Architecture in Scotland,* University of London Press, 1967.

INDEX

References to colour photographs appear in **bold**.